How to Create a Perfect School

How to Create a Perfect School

Maintain Students' *Motivation and Love of Learning* from Kindergarten through 12th Grade

LYLE LEE JENKINS

Foreword by Jack Canfield

ISBN: 978-1-956457-22-3 (paperback)
ISBN: 978-1-956457-35-3 (ebook)

Front cover photograph by Amanda Fish Photography, Omaha, Nebraska

Angela Willnerd, first grade teacher in Fremont, Nebraska, uses math manipulatives to illustrate effect sizes to her students. The four cubes in her left hand represent the average effect size of .40 from over 250 influences upon student learning. She uses this visual to explain that an effect size of .80 is double the learning of a .40, an effect size of 1.20 is triple the learning of a .40 and so on. The 23 cubes in Mrs. Willnerd's right hand represent almost six times the average learning from classrooms utilizing the processes explained in *How to Create a Perfect School*.

Cover and interior design by Christy Collins, Constellation Book Services

Printed in the United States of America

This book is dedicated to my two sons, Todd Jenkins and Jim Jenkins. They are wonderful sons, but more importantly, they both are amazing fathers.

TABLE OF CONTENTS

LIST OF FIGURES

FOREWORD

Anyone who has read *The Success Principles*™ knows that I am a firm believer in the power of visualization. What Lee Jenkins has visualized for education is a vibrant improvement for all students at all grade levels. Happily, the students also learn to visualize their progress, both as an individual and as a member of classrooms and whole schools. This is really, really important work in creating environments where students love to learn.

I know from a personal level as a student and a former high school teacher how much Lee Jenkins' book, *How to Create a Perfect School,* is needed in America and around the world. It is well known that something is not right with far too many schools. Maybe the best evidence that something is wrong is that today's educators are very often discouraging their own children and grandchildren from becoming the next generation of teachers.

At first I was a bit skeptical about the word "perfect," but once I understood the definition and the approaches Lee Jenkins writes and speaks about, I became a big supporter. Lee is now helping thousands of educators and I expect this will very soon become millions. His work is that powerful!

I love the structure of the book that first covers defining and measuring intrinsic motivation and then addresses the educational practices that destroy intrinsic motivation. Then he shows you how to replace these destructive practices with ones that create learning for learning's sake instead of learning for the test and then promptly forgetting what was learned. The book ends with "polishing perfect" using real classroom examples and supporting data. This section brings a huge smile to my heart. After reading it, I wanted to say, "Lee, where have you been all of my life?"

And this is a book for more than educators. If you are a business leader, I strongly encourage you to jump on the chance to have Dr. Jenkins work with the schools in your community. You all have lamented that students and graduates do not seem to know how to cooperate in the work place. The fact is that all of the constant competition for grades has not prepared them to become productive employees. Lee has the solutions you want for your community.

–Jack Canfield, Coauthor of *The Success Principles*™ and the *Chicken Soup for the Soul*® Series

PREFACE

The problem with most improvement suggestions is every one of them ducks the responsibility of management.

W. Edwards Deming

The first step in any organizational improvement plan is defining *perfect*. Once perfect is agreed upon, next comes determining where the organization's strengths and weaknesses fall.

Obviously, the organization is not perfect and thus there is a gap between perfect and current reality. The gap between current reality and perfect is where planning for improvement begins. What can be done together that has a strong possibility of moving the organization closer to perfect? What can be removed from the organization that is sabotaging the desire to move closer to perfect? What small adjustments can be made to the positive processes that will move the organization even closer to perfect?

You have just read the structure of *How to Create a Perfect School*.

Without defining what perfect looks like for a specific organization, most organizational planning results in a hurricane, a monsoon, or a blizzard. Ideas come and go based upon who has power at the moment. Consistency and even the ability to collect data on the effectiveness of procedures are hindered. People caught in one of these man-made disasters want somebody, anybody, to "fix" the organization. The next "fix" is far too often a tsunami.

Defining perfect is essential for lasting improvement in education. Ruthlessly erasing destructive policies, regardless of what was done in the past or what tradition says, is essential for growth. But more importantly, creating systems and procedures that are research-based and classroom-tested is required if lasting change is truly desired.

ACKNOWLEDGEMENTS

"God is in the business of strategically positioning us in the right place at the right time" (Batterson, 2006, p. 12). This book began in 1967 when God strategically placed me at the end-of-the-year faculty breakfast next to Evelyn Neufeld. She invited me to visit her classroom the next year. Until she left our school two years later to teach at San Jose State University, I observed in her classroom almost every day. My current work as author, speaker and consultant began because of Evelyn's influence.

Next Peggy McLean was hired to teach next door and she restored my love of science, plus co-authored a number of books, beginning with our first one entitled *It's A Tangram World*. Today she is the author of math quizzes which are so powerful in the lives of many children. (They are located at www.LBellJ.com)

Peggy and I were able to meet Mary Laycock because of our writing. The square root/cube root pattern is only one of many unusual, powerful strategies for mathematics Mary taught me. I asked her once how she learned so much math. She said that her roommate in college was also a math major. They proved every problem they were assigned two ways – once using algebra and once using geometry.

The fourth major influence on my life that is reflected in this book is Marion Nordberg. She taught a K-3 combination. It was in her classroom that my son asked for "caveman" as his first word to read in school. Marion balanced out my knowledge of mathematics with writing/reading expertise. She had 300-500 visitors each year to observe her classroom.

Then along came Bill Martin Jr. Over the years we worked together over 50 days. His influence and determination to never sacrifice between joy in learning and success in learning is apparent in *How to Create a Perfect School*.

Vic Cottrell came into my life because I couldn't answer one of his interview questions well. He asked what gave me the greatest joy as an administrator and I said, "Watching the growth of teachers and other adults." He said I was correct in understanding that the job of administrators is to help adults so they can be of even more help to students. However, the job is not to "watch" but to "help." Because he clarified my thinking, I knew he had so much to offer and I was right. One of many influences Vic had on my life was the feedback form mentioned in Chapter 22.

In 1990 I was standing in the hallway at an AASA conference when Lew Rhodes suggested what session I go to next. There, for the first time, I heard about W. Edwards Deming. The whole LtoJ process and every view of the whole system, such as the Jenkins Curve, is an outgrowth of what I learned from Deming.

If Jessica Allen of Corwin Press had not worked with me to publish *Optimize Your School* I would not have ever met John Hattie and learned that one of the graphs Deming taught me had all of the data necessary to calculate effect sizes. I have stated elsewhere in *How to Create a Perfect School* the other influences of John Hattie on my work and this book.

Steve and Laura Harrison urged me to meet with Jack Canfield. They knew him well and understood how much he would love the *How to Create a Perfect School* thesis and solutions. They were right and Jack offered to write the foreword.

Mark Batterson is right. God is in the business of strategically placing us at the right place at the right time. He is not done yet as you will realize as you read about the present.

God is not done. Currently I am so appreciative of Codi Hrouda and Allan Culp. These two teachers have consistently implemented my ideas. "Will this work?" I ask them. They not only tell me a 'yes' or 'no', but improve on each and every idea.

Several years ago I noticed in John Maxwell's acknowledgements that he stated he has a "writer." Interesting. Well, I have a writer in Adrienne Gain. Prior to sending of *How to Create a Perfect School* to Christopher Hoffman, editor, Adrienne read, edited and reworked every chapter. In addition, her husband, Jason, is my tech support. The effect size calculator and just about everything I do that involves a computer or video camera Jason has improved.

I hope all readers learn from the dichotomous rubrics in Chapter 24. The designers of these rubrics put a great deal of thought into each one of these. They are not easy to create. Thanks to all of these educators.

Martha Bullen is a colleague of Steve and Laura Harrison with Bradley Communication. She has guided me step by step on the process of self-publishing—a first-time, but exhilarating experience. She recommended book designers and editors, and was involved with every aspect of both front and back covers. Her caring attitude bleeds from every suggestion.

Christy Collins' work as the book designer was impressive indeed. She designed the front and back covers plus completed all of the layout typesetting of the whole book. She came to this project with the eyes of an expert and the heart of a mother. What could be a better combination?

A year ago I wrote Angela Willnerd asking her to experiment with a couple of Grade 1 students with the effect size calculator. Could students this young enter the data into the spreadsheet? The answer was yes. Then she sent me the photo of her explaining effect size to her Grade 1 students. Wow! I was impressed. So, after receiving advice from both Martha and Christy, it was determined that this would be a great book cover. Amanda Fish was hired to professionally photograph Angela and students for the cover you have seen. If you need a photographer anywhere near Omaha, Nebraska, contact Amanda Fish photography.

I am so thankful for the three endorsements on the back cover. Julie Otero, David Hurst and John Hattie put considerable thought into how to communicate thoughts in a few words. They were so successful. Further, John Hattie is the one who gave the name "Jenkins Curve" to figure 2.2.

And then there is Jack Canfield. What can I say? After interviewing me for 45 minutes off camera and then again for the video located at www.LBellJ.com, Jack asked if I would like to have him write the foreword for *How to Create a Perfect School*. By now you have read the superb foreword. In addition he adjusted my previous draft book title to what is now in print. It is not an accident that Jack has authored more non-fiction books than anyone ever; he is pure genius. Obviously, I am very grateful for his assistance.

Introduction

It is theoretically possible for a child to be highly intrinsically motivated and still perform poorly. But the number of such students, I warrant, will never be great.

Alfie Kohn

The principles, research, and ideas explored in *How to Create a Perfect School* are presented for one and only one reason: it will be nearly impossible to make dramatic improvements in education as long as year after year more and more students put in less effort and receive less and less joy from their schooling.

The hard news is that perfect cannot be bought, but it can be taught. No matter what is promoted through marketing or politics, perfect is not for sale.

The good news is that perfect is free. It is called intrinsic motivation and arrives inside our kindergartners. *How to Create a Perfect School* is written to maintain this free asset of intrinsic motivation and then to polish it.

Almost all students bring with them to kindergarten all the intrinsic motivation they need for life. In a perfect school these students keep their intrinsic motivation for the next 12 years. Society has no idea what could happen in schools all over the world if students maintained this motivation to learn all 13 years of kindergarten to twelfth-grade education. Currently, in the United States, 5-8% of the students are intrinsically motivated to learn in high school. Yes, approximately 40% of these students love school, but it is for athletics, trips, and friends—not for the actual learning.

> **When people are intrinsically motivated, they work really hard, and they love it.**

When people are intrinsically motivated, they work really hard, and they love it. In *How to Create a Perfect School*, this is labeled Will & Thrill. We measure and improve intrinsic motivation with two amazing tools: ears.

In order for education to fulfill its potential, parents, teachers, administrators, school board members, and legislators must agree on the definition of perfect. When students love school and put in 100% effort, learning takes care of itself. In fact, the teachers will complain that they don't have time to keep up with all the students want to learn. Every new initiative, policy, and law will be judged by the definition of perfect. Will the proposed initiative, policy, or law bring us closer to perfect? If not, will it keep us safer? If not, why are we considering it, anyway?

Friends and colleagues know that I have been immersed for some time in the writing of the book in your hand. When they ask, "What is the title of your new book?" I tell them, "How to Create a Perfect School." The obvious follow-up question is, "What is perfect?" I explain, and the response is always: "Yes, that would be perfect!" Next comes the question, "How can this be accomplished?"

How to Create a Perfect School includes the definition of perfect, plus measurement and feedback processes. The book then moves forward to proven strategies for moving schools closer and closer to perfect every week, month, quarter, and year. Hundreds of educators have assisted in refining these strategies over the years. Readers of *How to Create a Perfect School* will add many more refinements for years to come. We can do this.

The Prize = Perfect

Above all, keep your eye on the prize: intrinsic motivation.

Jessica Lahey

Defining perfect is the first step for a major improvement in any organization. Once perfect is defined, the next step is measuring where the organization is currently. A gap between perfect and current reality is to be expected. That is precisely what you will read in Part I—the definition of perfect, the process for measuring it, and then how to use ears to learn strategies for moving closer to perfect.

When educators who are parents and parents who are not educators express their dreams for their children, their aspirations are the same. John Hattie's book, *Visible Learning for Teachers*, explores this idea. In the book he quotes Paul Brock, his friend and fellow educator in Australia, who directs his daughters' teachers to: "nurture and challenge my daughters' intellectual and imaginative capacities way out to horizons unsullied by self-fulfilling minimalist expectations. Don't patronise them with lowest-common denominator blancmange* masquerading as knowledge and learning; nor crush their love for learning through boring pedagogy."

Hattie closes Brock's exhortation for educators with: "[S]urely this is what every parent and student should be able to expect of school education." Hattie and Conoghue give us the education triplets of skill, will and thrill (Hattie and Conoghue, 2016, p. 2). It is the will and thrill that

---

* Australian readers will all recognize this word. Others can imagine it is a synonym for nonsense.

Paul Brock does not want crushed. Then Hattie and Conoghue go on to write, "[F]urther work is needed to identify the strategies that optimize the dispositions (will) and the motivation (thrill) outcomes" (Hattie and Conoghue, p. 4). My hope is that *How to Create a Perfect School* will make a significant contribution to the identification of the needed strategies.

Perfect is within our reach; it is the prize.

CHAPTER 1

The First Day of Kindergarten

Try to encourage a kid to learn math by paying her for each workbook page she completes and she'll almost certainly become diligent in the short term and lose interest in the long term.

Daniel Pink

Bright-eyed adventurers cling to their protectors with shaky hands as they begin the next quest that will help guide them into adulthood. Jackson struts proudly in his new shoes, while Evelynn steals a glance at her reflection in the window, beaming at the stylish backpack from Grandma. Andrew's mother is doing her best to choke back emotion. Danny's nanna sheds a tear and Jenny's poor daddy has used up half the box of tissues they were asked to bring for the classroom supplies.

It is the first day of kindergarten. However, this particular day has a twist. The principal, Mrs. Anderson, has made arrangements to meet with the parents right after they walk away from the classroom. Provided for the parents is a cup of coffee, sweets, and a table with 25 index cards, one per family, face down. Each family is to randomly select one card. The cards are labeled: K, 1, 1, 2, 2, 3, 3, 4, 4, 5, 5, 6, 6, 7, 7, 8, 8, 9 sports, 9 friends, 10 sports, 10 music, 11 friends, 11 theater, 12 music, 12 learning.

Mrs. Anderson welcomes the families and then continues, "Each family has an index card with a letter or numeral and maybe also a word. Please, everyone, stand up. You now all represent the children who love to learn—100% of you. For the past five years you have sacrificed sleep, answered 'why' at least 10,000 times, read the same book over and over again, and helped them become independent thinkers, all to ensure that your child would have the best start in life. All of those tasks led you to this moment, dropping your child off for the first day of kindergarten.

"I am going to call out the numbers, letters, or words, one at a time. When I read the information on your card, I want you to sit down," directs the principal. As she reads, "K," for kindergarten, one parent is seated. Then as she reads, "One, two, three, four, five, six, seven, and eight," two parents sit down each time. Last of all she reads, "Nine friends, nine sports, ten music, ten sports, eleven friends, eleven theater, and twelve music."

"Now comes the sad reason for what we just did. Lee Jenkins surveyed 3,000 teachers, asking them two questions: What grade level do you teach and what percentage of your students love school? We all just enacted this research. As your grade level was chosen and you sat down, you represented students who started kindergarten loving school and now no longer love school. When we came to high school, the story expanded. When you sat down you represented a student who no longer loves learning, but does love school for friends, sports, music, or theater. Only one of all 25 students still loves learning. One family is still standing.

"Please do not go home discouraged or tempted to blame teachers. The teachers at the schools Dr. Jenkins surveyed were not discouraging learning in students on purpose. The teachers were working very hard. They were doing their best in a system that always discourages the majority of students. Always. You enrolled your child in one of the schools following the principles and practices outlined in Lee Jenkins' book *How to Create a Perfect School.* We endeavor every moment of every day to maintain, and even accelerate, the love of learning inside each of the kindergarten students you just entrusted us with. The Heath brothers wrote, 'You can't appreciate the solution until you appreciate the problem' (Heath and Heath, 2017, p. 106). This activity with the cards was done to give you an appreciation of the problem we are addressing and improving every day.

"Throughout the next few years you will learn precisely (1) some traditional practices that discourage students that we have replaced with ones that provide joy in learning and (2) that we rely greatly upon listening to students and parents. Perfect would be every parent having an index card with '12 learning.' In fact, as you leave, I will give you a '12 learning' index card. Put this on your refrigerator so we can remember where we are all going together for the next 13 years. Our goal is to celebrate with 100% of our students remaining as enthused about learning as they are now."

As Mrs. Anderson watched, the parents pack up their belongings and glance at their index cards. Next month they would meet again to share their stories and learn tips to preserve their students' intrinsic motivation.

CHAPTER 2

Is Perfect Really Possible?

People are asking for better schools, with no clear idea of how to improve education, nor even how to define improved education.

W. Edwards Deming

Children are born with the motivation to learn. Psychologists call this inner drive to learn *intrinsic motivation*; it comes from within. When somebody attempts to motivate another person through promises, fear, rewards, or companionship, psychologists label this *extrinsic motivation*; it comes from outside the individual. Intrinsic motivation is inside every human being from birth, unless another person, usually an adult, diminishes it. Almost all of these former babies arrive in kindergarten, five years later, with their intrinsic motivation in place. They are so eager to begin school!

Perfect is defined as a school where all students have maintained their intrinsic motivation in kindergarten and for 12 more years. Since there are some students who have maintained their intrinsic motivation through high school, readers may inquire how this happened. It seems that the students who have maintained their intrinsic motivation for 13 years have done so by habit. James Clear writes, "The ultimate form of intrinsic motivation is when a habit becomes part of your identity" (Clear, 2018, p. 33). As you read this book you will learn what schools do to develop these necessary habits.

The premise of *How to Create a Perfect School* and the reason for writing this book are a vision of what could happen in schools all over the world if students merely maintained the intrinsic motivation they were

Students will be pressuring teachers to teach more!

born with. *How to Create a Perfect School* will experience no limit to what it can accomplish in every country. No limit. Early in my career, Mary Laycock instilled the basics of what you are reading. She wrote, "[W]e came to believe that it was our personal and professional responsibility to make mathematics for children meaningful, exciting, pleasant and enjoyable. We were appalled at the number of children who were learning to dislike numbers and, therefore, to dislike the teachers of numbers" (Laycock and Watson, 1975, p. 1).

Instead of teachers complaining that these students are unmotivated, the teachers will complain that there just is not enough time to keep up with all that the students want to learn! Students will be pressuring teachers to teach more! Students in *A Perfect School* classrooms are making this a reality. They are working extremely hard and yet receive great joy from the tasks teachers assign them, even if those tasks are challenging.

Intrinsic motivation, for the purpose of *How to Create a Perfect School*, is a blending of effort and joy. When students are intrinsically motivated, they work exceptionally hard because they want to, and because they receive great joy from the learning. In *How to Create a Perfect School*, I am using John Hattie's triplets of Skill, Will and Thrill. Skill is measured separately from Will and Thrill. Section III describes Skill measurement. In Part I will focus only upon Will and Thrill.

Figure 2.1, the logo for the LtoJ process, to be explained in Part III, displays the distance between perfect and an estimate of where schools are now in maintaining intrinsic motivation. I find no difference in this regard between public, private, and charter schools. Compare the large space of the 12-sided dodecagon with the small space inside the letter O. The large space represents

Fig. 2.1

the number of kindergartners who are intrinsically motivated to learn, and the space inside the letter *O* represents the number of Grade 12 students who still have this intrinsic motivation——5-8% of high school seniors are still intrinsically motivated to learn.

This comes from the survey represented in figure 2.2 that John Hattie renamed The Jenkins Curve. The percentage of students in high school who still love school is an indication of intrinsic motivation. The number hovers around 40%. Further questioning reveals, however, that only 5-8% of high school students love school learning. Other high school students who say they love school are thinking of the extracurricular or cocurricular activities. (Cocurricular activities are often connected to music and theatre. The content is taught in class, but then there are productions, which often involve travel, connected to the classroom instruction.)

Fig. 2.2

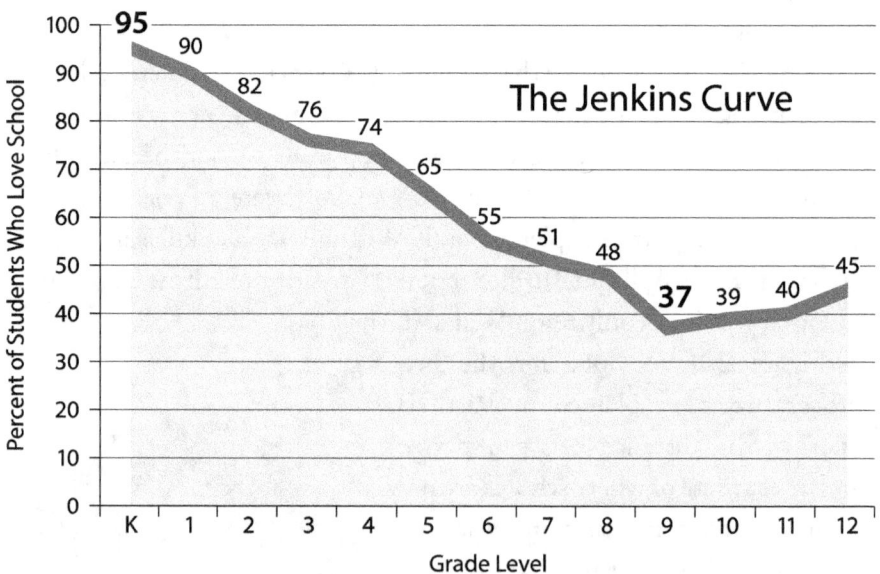

All organizations have a gap between perfect and current reality. Even the major airlines, who are as close to having a perfect safety record as any organization, have a gap. Although I describe the gap in intrinsic motivation as being between 5% and 100%, this book is not written pessimistically. *How to Create a Perfect School* is a hopeful, positive book, describing how schools can move closer and closer to perfect and how parents can be the best partners in this journey.

> **If intrinsic motivation in students between kindergarten and Grade 12 was maintained, almost all of the problems schools face would disappear**

If intrinsic motivation in students between kindergarten and Grade 12 was maintained, almost all of the problems schools face—low test scores, discipline problems, high absentee rates, tardiness and bullying—would disappear. I want to place the tools needed to nurture intrinsic motivation into the hands of educators worldwide. To do this we must discuss how to measure intrinsic motivation in the first place.

A word of caution is appropriate here: when people read about this loss of enthusiasm for school learning, their tendency is to find people to blame. Please do not. The blame falls on the system, and by that I do not mean bureaucracy; I mean the culture around how school is supposed to operate. Already there are many teachers who are successful at maintaining and even accelerating students' intrinsic motivation. But once the year is over, the students are cast back into a system that systematically decelerates intrinsic motivation. I suggest that readers look at the Jenkins Curve again. It is obvious that no single teacher, no grade level, and no secondary department can solve this loss of enthusiasm for school; management must lead the effort.

CHAPTER 3

How in the World Can Perfect be Measured?

The purpose of feedback is to reduce the gap between current and desired states of knowing.

John Hattie and Gregory Yates

"We can't just sit back and wait for feedback to be offered, particularly when we're in a leadership role. If we want feedback to take root in the culture, we need to explicitly ask for it." Ed Batista spoke these words and he could not be more correct. With feedback comes improvement, and who better to give feedback than the students themselves? If we ask students for their opinions, they are eager to share ways they think their own education can improve.

Even students who are frequently referred to the office for discipline problems come up with creative, positive ideas when asked their opinions on how to improve their school. Asking about intrinsic motivation is no different.

Figure 3.1 documents students' descriptions of their effort and joy in regard to learning. When students are asked to provide feedback regarding their effort and joy, it causes them to think about their feelings in ways they have not considered before. Both the students and the teachers receive valuable feedback from this simple process. The students see how their effort and joy compares to the feedback of classmates, and the teacher sees the class as a whole. Instead of teachers being concerned about a lack of student motivation and having no recourse, they have tangible data from which to improve motivation.

Fig. 3.1

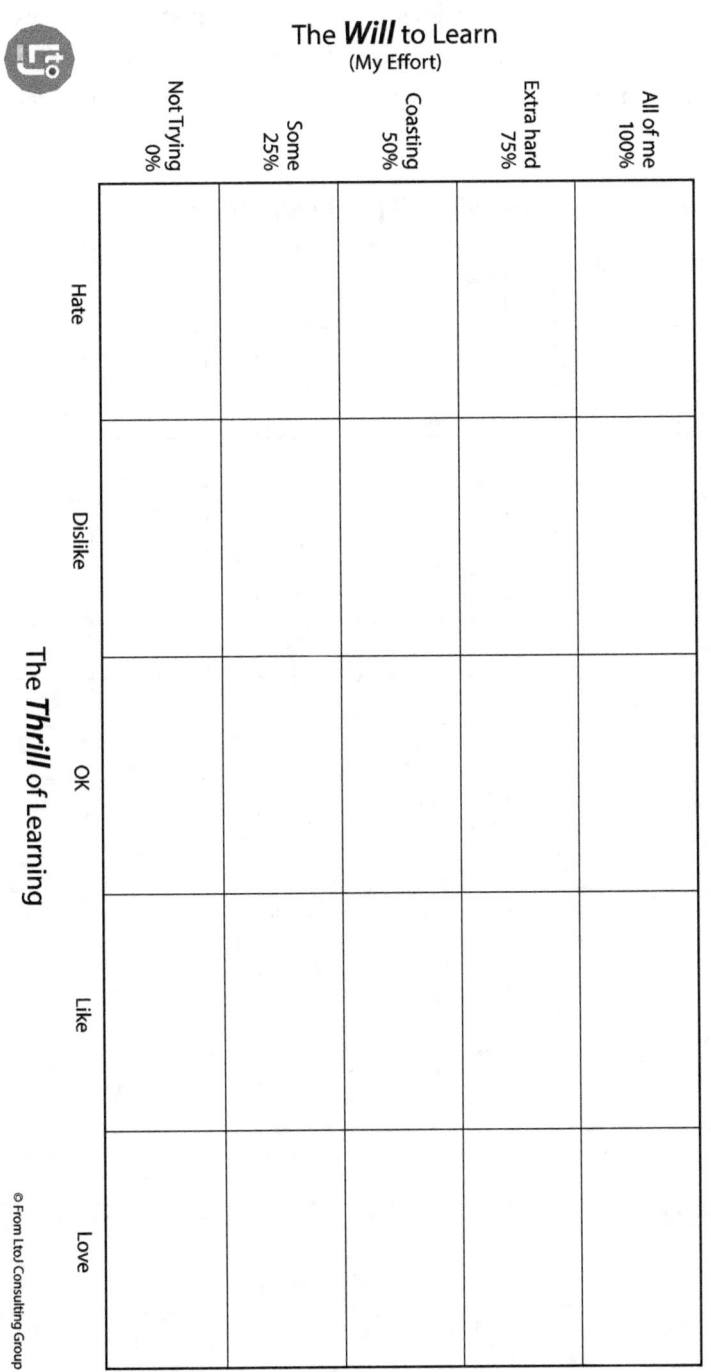

The **Will** to Learn
(My Effort)

Will & Thrill Matrix

The **Thrill** of Learning

© From LtoJ Consulting Group

The process for gathering the data for the Will & Thrill Matrix is to provide each student with a mini-matrix. After each student places their single dot on the mini-matrix, (figure 3.2), a couple of students record these dots on a full size matrix, (figure 3.1). Fifteen mini-matrices have

Fig. 3.2   ## Mini Will & Thrill Matrices

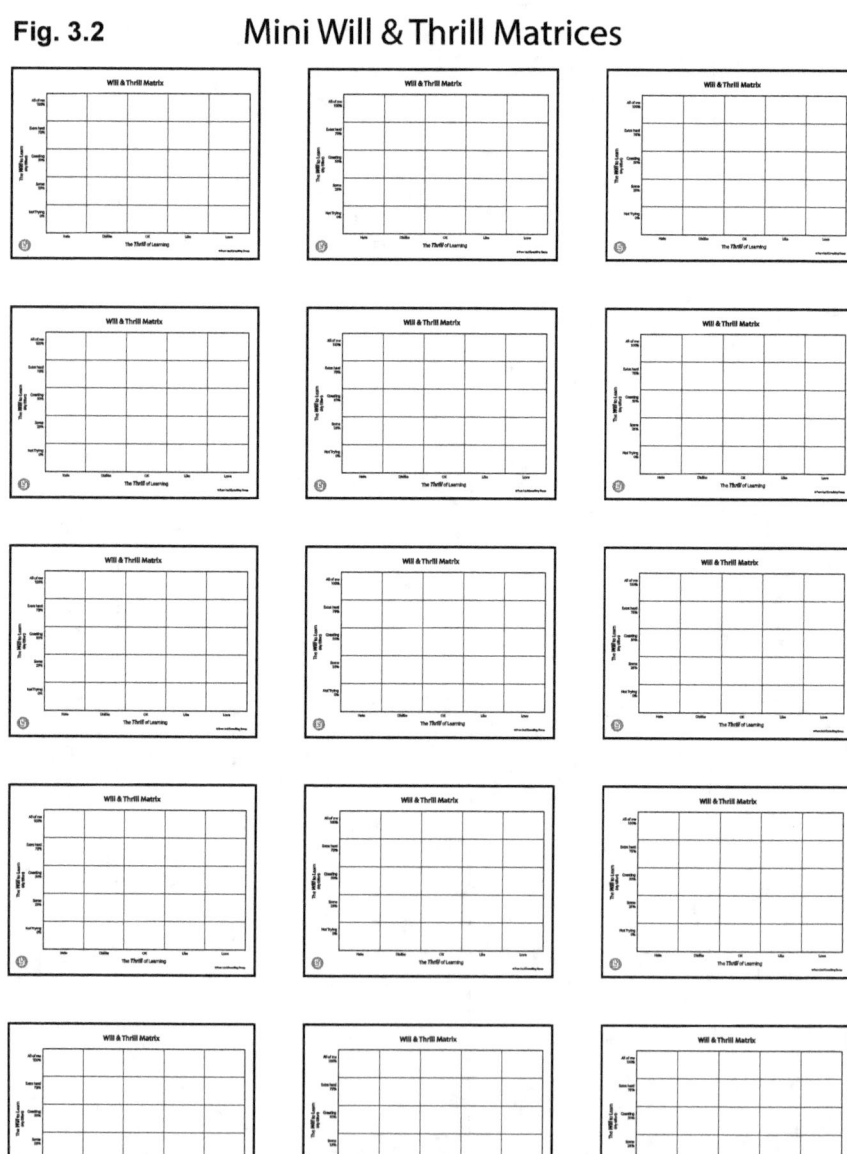

been placed on one page, which is available to download from the *How to Create a Perfect School* resources located at www.LBellJ.com/perfect.

Figure 3.3 is an example of the Will & Thrill Matrix from Allan Culp's Grade 7 social studies classrooms. Matrices like this one provide insight for students and teachers regarding intrinsic motivation. Teachers and students alike can quickly ascertain whether students are putting in their full effort, doing just enough to get by, or not putting forth any effort. They can also determine whether students are feeling the thrill of learning or not. Some teachers may find that the feedback tends to be negative, with lots of dislikes and hates. The temptation to blame students in these classrooms must be avoided. Every subject and every grade level has teachers who struggle to either connect with the content or connect with their students. The Will & Thrill Matrix gives students a safe place to voice their dislike without singling them out and informs the teacher of areas where they may be able to improve in order to increase student effort and enjoyment. Of course, what all teachers want to see is a preponderance of dots moving towards maximum effort and love for learning. By using the Will & Thrill Matrix regularly, they are able to collect data in order to do just that. No matter what the dots communicate, this is the feedback Batista was referring to in the above quotation.

Fig. 3.3

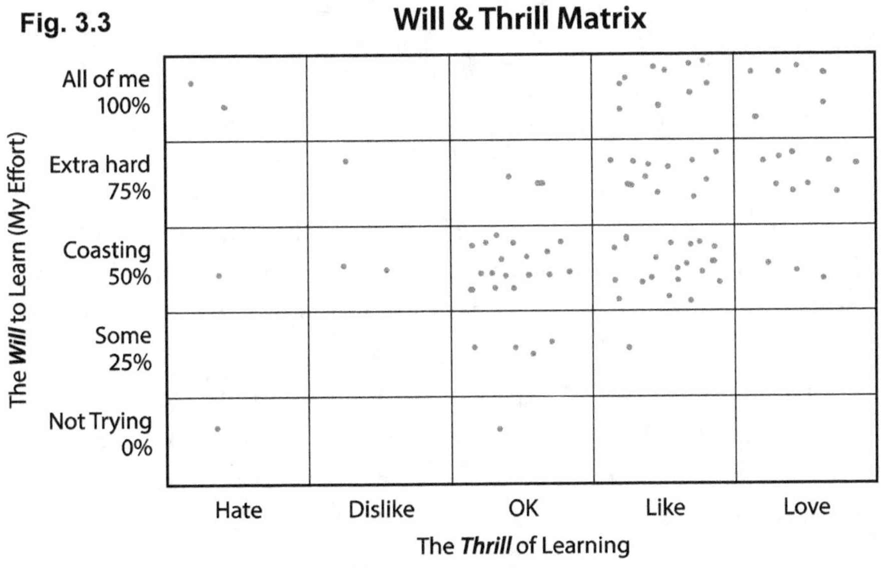

Will & Thrill Matrix

The *Thrill* of Learning

> **Educators with a growth mindset are interested in maintaining, at times restoring, and even accelerating intrinsic motivation.**

Educators with a growth mindset are interested in maintaining, at times restoring, and even accelerating intrinsic motivation.

Figure 3.4 shows the numerical value given to each cell on the Will & Thrill Matrix. Students count the value of each dot on the matrix, calculate the average score and report the results to the teacher and their classmates. The goal is to move closer to the ideal score of 9 on the matrix, representing 100% effort and a love of learning.

Fig. 3.4

Will & Thrill Matrix

The *Will* to Learn (My Effort)		Hate	Dislike	OK	Like	Love
All of me	100%	5	6	7	8	9
Extra hard	75%	4	5	6	7	8
Coasting	50%	3	4	5	6	7
Some	25%	2	3	4	5	6
Not Trying	0%	1	2	3	4	5

The *Thrill* of Learning

Figure 3.5 shows the work performed by two students calculating Codi Hrouda's Grade 5 intrinsic motivation score. Even the act of scoring intrinsic motivation requires students to learn how to interpret and analyze numerical data. They are actively involved in their own education.

The final step in receiving feedback regarding intrinsic motivation is to receive ideas from the students regarding how to improve student Will and student Thrill. The improvement process is rooted in advice provided by students.

Fig. 3.5   **Will & Thrill Matrix**

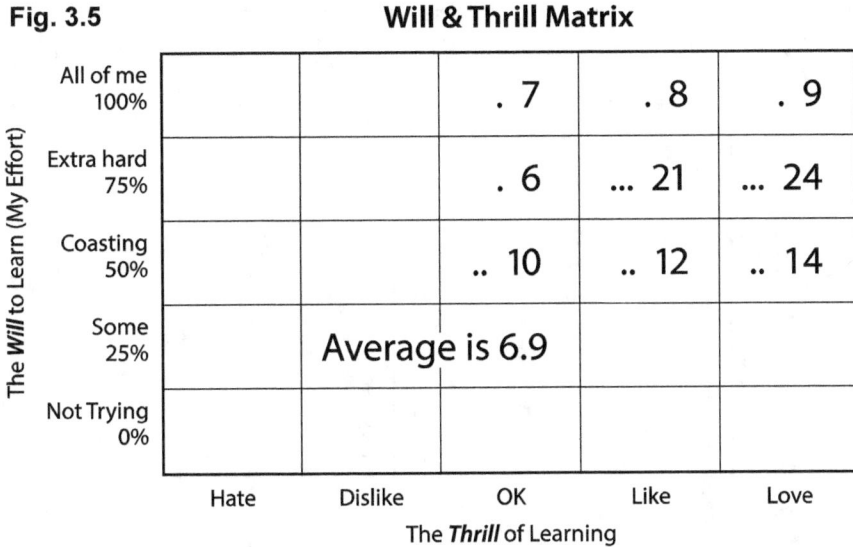

Figure 3.6 is the feedback form used to gain insights from students regarding their motivation. With all suggestion forms I strongly recommend that teachers tell the students two things: (1) they will read every form, and (2) they will do their very best to make at least one change per month based upon student input. If this is not stated up front, students naturally think the teachers can or should implement all the different suggestions. While it is not possible to implement all of the suggestions, teachers have the opportunity to choose at least one suggestion to experiment with and find out if the students' suggestions actually improve effort and joy. This simple statement allows students to be part of an active team invested in their own education, instead of sitting back as passive recipients of decisions made without their input.

Let's all listen to the students and their feedback. In spite of being an obvious lover of classic books for high school students, in his book *Classics in the Classroom*, Michael Clay Thompson writes, "Each pedagogical decision must be evaluated in terms of the effect it will have on the kids' love of the book. If this emphasis of students over books seems inconsistent with a reverence for the classics, remember that it is no favor to the classics to teach people to hate them" (Thompson, 1995, p. 38).

Fig. 3.6

Will & Thrill Feedback

This helped me work harder:	This helped me enjoy learning more:
This might help us work harder:	This might help us enjoy learning more:

Fig. 3.7 **Allan Culp's Grade 7 History Will & Thrill**
2017–18

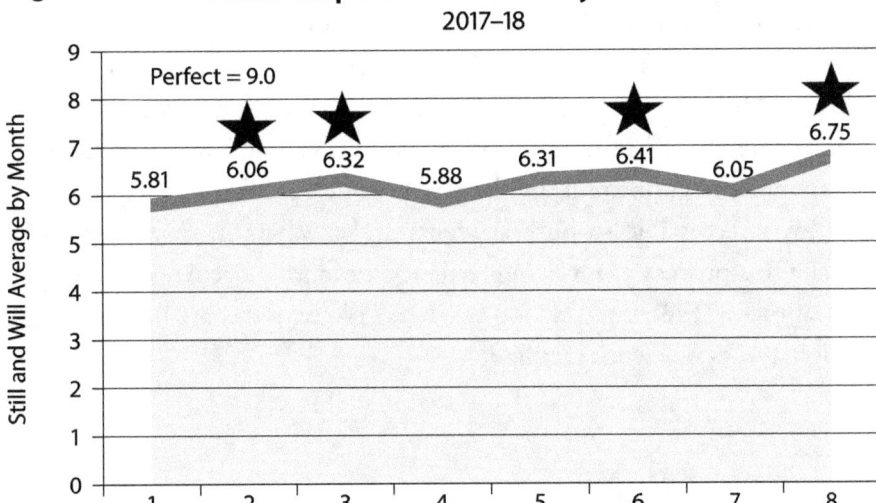

Figure 3.7 is the record of effort and joy over the course of one school year from Allen Culp's Grade 7 social studies classes. Stars indicate the four best months that year. It is important for students and teachers to recognize when improvement is occurring.

Figure 3.6 reflects only the social studies class and is not reflective of students' attitudes towards all of their classes. By contrast, Figure 3.4 pertains to the whole elementary-school classroom experience. However, elementary teachers also have the choice to ask for feedback for only one subject.

It is worth noting that in Figure 3.5, a 5 is the highest possible score with only one aspect of the Will & Thrill Matrix. This 5 would be either a student who hated the course but put forth maximum effort or a student who loved the course, but put forth no effort. Both effort and joy are essential; education is not to be an either/or experience.

When teachers take the time to ask students for input, they are often surprised at the simplicity of the advice. Shelly Craig received this advice from a student in her Grade 11 history class: "When you promise us 10 minutes, give us 10 minutes." Shelly went back to her class the next day and said, "Somebody wrote, 'When you promise us 10 minutes, give us 10 minutes.' Don't I do this already?" In unison, the class said, "No." Shelly asked, "What do I do?" The students said, "Mrs. Craig, you are hyper. After about seven minutes you can't take it anymore and tell us time is up." Shelly replied, "What should I do about this?" The students responded, "Let one of us be the timekeeper." Problem solved.

Joy is accessible to both students and teachers in classrooms who make this process of receiving feedback a monthly occurrence. Let's call this process "Hearing Aids for Teachers." No batteries are necessary; the original ears will work just fine.

CHAPTER 4

Are These Kids Telling Me the Truth?

Sampling increased the accuracy of the results, and saved much time and effort in tabulation.

W. Edwards Deming

In the 2016 United States presidential election, a new method for collecting poll predictions was tested on voters. Survey participants were asked to predict whom they believed their neighbors, close friends, or relatives would vote for in the election. This method, called social-circle polling, resulted in more accurate election results than previous surveys. "Why?" you may ask. Santa Fe Institute Professor Mirta Galesic explains, "People can be embarrassed to admit they plan to vote for a less popular candidate but are less embarrassed to say this about their friends. They also tend to know people in their social circles fairly well and can predict their voting habits (Galesic, 2018)." We use the same method for collecting data from students in *A Perfect School* classrooms.

Many say that schools will never fully reach perfection. This belief can color one's view of the data collection if one is not careful. It is tempting to think, "Since we will never be perfect, why bother wasting more time collecting data?" A better way to look at data collection and analyzation is, "Although we will never be perfect, together we can get closer each day, week, month, and year." Data collection and analytics are essential in measuring the effectiveness of the processes and strategies outlined in *How to Create a Perfect School*.

Most teachers at some point during the school year will wonder, "Are the students telling me the truth about the effort they are exerting and the joy they feel in my class?" Data collection allows teachers to take a snapshot of their class's joy and effort using the Will & Thrill matrix.

But the data collection only goes so far. By using the social-circle method teachers can prove whether or not students are answering truthfully on the Will & Thrill Matrix.

Social-Circle Polling of Classrooms Using the Will & Thrill Matrix:

1. Randomly select five or six students from a class of 20 to 35 pupils. If measuring a university or other course with more students, use the square root of the total number of scholars as the approximate number of participants to randomly select. (e.g. 81 students, square root = nine students)

2. Ask each student to write down the names of five other students in the class that they know well. Inform them that the teacher will not be collecting the names.

3. Provide each selected student with a blank Will & Thrill Matrix. Ask the students to place five dots on the matrix that represent what they believe about the effort and joy expressed by each of the five students they chose in step 2. The students are not to place a dot for themselves.

4. Choose two students to place all dots from the individual matrices onto one social-circle matrix, creating a complete picture of intrinsic motivation for the classroom.

5. Have these have students calculate the average number of points from the social-circle matrix using the 1–9 scale provided in Figure 3.4.

6. Compare the average number of points from the social-circle matrix with the average from a recently completed classroom Will & Thrill Matrix.

7. If the difference between the average scores of the social-circle matrix and the classroom matrix is more than one point off on the 1–9 scale, set aside time for a classroom discussion or quick writing assignment that explores why the two matrices differ.

"Good leaders motivate others by their listening skills" (Maxwell, 2007, p. 1544). When teachers take the time to ensure the dots on the Will & Thrill Matrix are accurate, they are essentially becoming better leaders by listening more to their students. Teachers never want to assume there is great joy in the classroom when in actuality students loathe attending each class period. They also do not want to be fooled into thinking students are working hard, when students are merely doing enough to pass each class. Double-checking truly reinforces the students' perception that they have a listening leader as a teacher.

When educators accept the premise that students' intrinsic motivation is the most powerful force within schools and then measure it, they are well on their way to truly improving schools.

Schools will never be perfect, with all students putting forth maximum effort and loving every aspect of education. Nevertheless, all professional educators have a responsibility to empower their students. Imagine what scholars in our schools could accomplish if they harnessed their will to work hard, received great joy from the learning process, and were led by teachers that listen to student input. The possibilities are endless.

CHAPTER 5

Perfect for Parents

*If there's any trick to parenting, it is to keep our children
from losing that internal drive.*

Jessica Lahey

The room was buzzing with conversation as the kindergarten parents congregated around steaming cups of coffee and tea. Principal Anderson slowly glided through the room catching pieces of conversations as she went. "Oh, I hear you!" said a small but very expressive blonde woman. "I looked everywhere to get one of those last Christmas, and do you know how long he was entertained? Four hours. I'm telling you, my son finds more excitement in rocks and sticks than in all these expensive toys they've got out on the market." A few feet away there was a large man in a business suit speaking with a slightly smaller man in athletic gear. "You just never know what to expect with little girls, one minute she's playing tea parties and dress up and the next it's raspberry blowing contests! I grew up with three brothers; I was not prepared for this." Principal Anderson smiled and glanced at a pair of moms quietly chatting in the corner. "Oh, I agree, there is nothing as exhausting as being a mother. But you know, one of the best feelings is watching your child find their sense of wonder. I remember a day when I was just fed up with Jackson, he had made a mess of the living room with baby powder, and I had scolded him and pulled out the vacuum to have him help me clean up. After we got the room back in order, he started asking me questions about how the vacuum works. I pulled up a few videos and we watched them together.

When his dad got home it was all he could talk about! You just never know what will inspire them."

Once Principal Anderson completed her lap around the room, she called the group to order.

She started the meeting by saying, "I heard several interesting stories as I was walking around the room just now. It seems you could share with each other for hours. Hopefully, new adult friendships begin developing as we meet each month."

She continued, "Over the summer I read Jessica Lahey's book entitled *The Gift of Failure*. She wrote, 'If there's any trick to parenting, it is to keep our children from losing that internal drive.' You parents have protected your child's drive to learn for five years prior to the start of kindergarten, so you know the trick Lahey writes about in her book. You answered the question 'Why?' 10,000 times without saying something harmful. You joined in your child's wonder as they discovered something new. I overheard one of you share how your son became interested in how a vacuum cleaner worked. You let them play with the empty boxes, pots and pans, or sticks and stones instead of the new whiz-bang toy grandma and grandpa purchased. You have an almost perfect child, who admittedly melts down sometimes, but loves to absorb new knowledge and is excited to be in school learning more daily.

"Today I will provide three ideas to help all of us continue to preserve our students' intrinsic motivation. Hopefully, at least one of these ideas will slide easily into the normal activities of your family.

> **Do not overlook as insignificant the hurts that harm this internal drive.**

1. **Monitor effort and joy regularly.** The best indicators for the preservation of internal drive are hard work and joy in learning. When our internal drive is in high gear to learn more, these elements—effort and joy—are in place. We work hard and enjoy it. The goal is to continue to see your child express

joy in learning, even as kindergarten, and school in general, become more difficult. When you engage in conversation with your child, help them make sense of difficult items. When learning makes sense, students can end every learning task with joy. With *A Perfect School* techniques, you should see the spark of joy and will to do better every day. If you should see a consistent lessening of effort or joy, please let us know.

2. **Acknowledge the big and ignore the small.** Do not overlook as insignificant the hurts that harm this internal drive. Lee Jenkins received an email from a teacher in one of his seminars that said, "For 30 years I thought I was dumb. That's because there was a sticker chart on the wall in kindergarten and I couldn't get as many stickers as my friends." That is a biggie; we will work together to eliminate the biggies. These are the things that deter your children from learning. Maybe it's embarrassment, like the example I just shared. Maybe it's boredom, or feeling incompetent with the material. Whatever it is, do not forget that it is a big deal that your child's intrinsic motivation be protected and that their frustrations are acknowledged. On that note, let your child deal with the little bumps along the way on their own. There will be little issues. You child will have to learn how to problem solve, manage disappointments, and persevere. Parents should acknowledge the little issues for the moment and support their children as they learn. Understand that when 20 or more people are placed in a small space there will be issues. Your children can learn to handle these. Actually, I think 20 children in a 10-square-meter room get along better than 20 adults in the same amount of space.

3. **Respect.** Adults should not have a process in place for children that they would not want for themselves. Think about the sticker chart. We do not have sticker charts in the faculty room displaying the progress or lack thereof of teachers with dots after their names. Know this about child psychol-

ogy. Children do not think like adults, but they feel the exact same emotions as adults. If an adult is defending a harmful comment by saying, 'It's okay, they are only children,' help this adult know basic child psychology. Children's emotions and experiences deserve to be respected. This is how they learn to respect others and to respect their educational journey. Put into practice the golden rule; treat children as you would like to be treated.

"Finally, thank anyone inconvenienced because of your attending this meeting. Please do not ever forget the dream you had for your child the first day of kindergarten. Remember to pick up a copy of the three suggestions on your way out.

> **Children do not think like adults, but they feel the exact same emotions as adults.**

See you in a month." As the parents gathered their belongings and shuffled out of the classroom, the chatter between them resumed. Principal Anderson overheard two parents debriefing the meeting.

"Wow, how refreshing to not hear about behavior expectations or homework," one parent said. "Or about test scores, either," the other replied.

Mrs. Anderson smiled to herself, excited for the future that lay ahead for these kindergarten students, and the ones to come after them. With the parents on board, they were heading in the right direction for a perfect school.

Pass by the Path to Perfect and You Will Be Perplexed in the Province of Imperfect

*A habit is a behavior that has been repeated
enough times to become automatic.*

James Clear

The path that moves schools closer and closer to perfect every day, week, month, quarter, and year unfortunately involves removing bad habits from schools. As long as schools continue to add elements without subtracting harmful behaviors, they will never find the path towards perfect. Part II of *How to Create a Perfect School* details practices that have become so automatic in schools that they are assumed to be the way school is supposed to be.

Unfortunately, these practices combine to destroy students' intrinsic motivation. My job is to help both educators and parents to trip over and remove these very harmful habits.

"Sometimes we have to start by unlearning what we already know so that correct and more powerful learning can take place" (Hattie and Yates, 2014, p. 114). Hattie and Yates have given us the mindset necessary for avoiding the Province of Imperfect. Unlearning is necessary.

Educators often hear the words *teaching* and *learning* together. I never want to diminish teaching, but maybe the words should be *teaching* and *LEARNING*. Schools must remove some of the teaching habits that diminish learning; this is very hard. "Half of learning is learning. The

Schools must remove some of the teaching habits that diminish learning; this is very hard.

other half of learning is unlearning. Unfortunately, unlearning is twice as hard as learning" (Batterson, 2006, p. 44).

When educators read these words, the temptation is to be defensive. Please don't be. W. Edwards Deming loved to ask, "Who has the most control over a ship crossing the ocean?" Audience members would guess the captain, navigator, or engine-room boss. He happily stated that all of those answers are wrong. The person with the most control over the ship crossing the ocean is the one who designed the ship; it will never do better than it was designed to do. The individuals who designed our current education system are long gone. This system leaves worn-out teachers, unenthusiastic students, and confused parents in the ashes of the education experience.

So, who has the most control over education? It may very well be the people who created the weekly spelling test and the chapter test. Education's demotivating habits have been around for a long time. Before we embark on the next initiative, Tony Byrk has insight for us: "We often jump to implement a policy or programmatic change before fully understanding the exact problem to be solved" (Byrk, 2015, p. 468). Part II contains problems that must be solved in order to move out of the Province of Imperfect.

CHAPTER 6

How to Know What Will Be on the Test

Students might be told to remember, but appear to receive almost no guidance in how to remember.

Hattie and Yates

"How did you get an A on that test?" I asked, my mouth gaping as I stared over my friend's shoulder in my college statistics class. My friend had come to class a total of four times that month and yet there was a big, sharp A on his test. I, on the other hand, had never missed a class, spent hours studying, reviewed my notes, and worked harder in this class than in any other class. Yet I still was staring at a very curvy C. I was baffled. What was my friend doing that I was missing? His response left me even more confused.

"I figured out his formula. Every professor has a formula. They test you on what they think is important, not necessarily the material we are learning. Once you figure that out you don't really need to study. All you have to do is give them the answer they want."

Even though that was a few decades ago, I now know that I was not alone. In fact, students in the generations to follow had experiences similar to mine. They spent hours studying, reviewing notes, reading previous assignments, creating study groups, and paying hundreds of dollars to tutors. However, when exam grades were handed back, the grades were lower than expected. The same was not true for the students who had figured out the professors' and teachers' formulas. They glanced over the material once or twice, took the exams and received top scores. The outcome was not matching the effort. How could students enjoy or even comprehend what they were learning when they spent so much time trying to achieve the elusive A?

In an audience of teachers and administrators, I asked, "How many of you were able to figure out ahead of time what the professors were going to put on the exams when you were in school?" About a quarter of the audience raised their hand. Next, I asked one of the teachers how she figured out what would be on the test. The answer impressed me.

The teacher shared that in college she was in a study group. But instead of studying, the group focused on figuring out the formula. The group spent the first half of their study time sharing insights and observations about the professor. Once all participants agreed on what information they felt was most important to the professor, they studied and quizzed each other on only that material. Never mind trying to understand the actual material, or learning how to apply the knowledge; they were not going to be assessed on it anyway.

Learning is not the goal when using this strategy; it is to place in short-term memory precisely what is necessary to get a good grade. In my opinion, this strategy would score two or three points on the Will & Thrill Matrix. That's quite a distance from a perfect nine. Even worse, the students are paying for an education they are not receiving. What a waste of time and resources.

Obviously, there are differences between K–12 schools and universities. However, the similarity is striking. Education is made up of winners and losers. If you are a winner, congratulations, you have figured out the formula to get through school. And if you are the loser, good luck trying to get that A. The less we make school about learning, the less our students will learn. We will never have a perfect-nine school as long as the system dictates there must be winners and losers. Do you know a student, identified as a loser, who reports giving 100% effort and loving school?

I am not advocating all As as a gift. That reminds me of the disastrous participation-trophy experiment. As you read further you will notice that

I am encouraging very high standards with a clear path for all students to meet them. Part III of *How to Create a Perfect School* lays out this path. Chapter 13 removes the confusion

> ...learn means learn; it does not mean cram and forget.

over what students are to learn. Chapter 16 explains that learn means learn; it does not mean cram and forget. With this understanding, learning becomes valuable, both to the teacher and to the students. Instead of school being a year-long guessing game of what matters most to the teachers, it becomes an active learning environment in which students walk away with lasting knowledge. In order for this to happen, students need to be clear about what it is they are going to learn. Teacher clarity plays an important part in the success of our students.

According to John Hattie's *Visible Learning* research, located at VisibleLearningPlus.com, teacher clarity about learning objectives almost doubles learning. It is critical that students know at the beginning of the year what key surface-learning concepts they are going to learn. By stating these concepts up front, students are made aware of how previous knowledge will build on new knowledge. They do not have to figure out the formula because everything they are expected to learn is clearly stated. Surface-learning concepts are provided to students as a list with deep-learning extensions for each surface-learning item. There is more to teacher clarity than only telling students what they are to learn; lessons have to make sense. However, informing students about what they are going to learn over the duration of the course is the first step.

92–95% of our students no longer enjoy learning because they know it is a game of winners and losers. *How to Create a Perfect School* aims to forever erase the phenomenon of students trying to crack the obscure "formula." Instead of students trying to figure out what qualifies as trivial tidbits in contrast to essential knowledge according to their teacher's opinion, the teachers clearly state what students will learn at the beginning of the year, and return to this list repeatedly. Every student at the beginning of the course knows exactly what concepts will be tested. The guesswork is gone and the work of learning can commence uninhibited. This is just one of the issues that needs to be addressed in order to reconstruct the educational system. We also need to recreate how data are collected and assessed.

Once the information is gathered, how do we evaluate that students are actually learning? Can the very way we publish and post data in the classroom harm students' performance? The next chapter will delve into that very subject.

CHAPTER 7

Data are Like Baseball Bats

Burden always comes first; then vision.

John Maxwell

Teachers spend hours planning out the perfect bulletin board with the perfect theme to motivate students. A United States football field should do the trick. Everybody loves football. Right? First spend hours searching Pinterest, researching how to make the field look as realistic as possible. Then cut out a helmet for each student, careful to not cut off the face guard. Grab a good permanent marker and write each student's name on a helmet. Make the letters large so that every student can read their name from across the room. After putting up the football-field bulletin board, explain the process to students. Yardage toward a touchdown will be awarded for satisfactorily completing specified assignments. Finally, sit back and watch all your students excel this year.

If we were to observe the classroom two weeks after this touchdown process begins, what do you think we would find? I can tell you without even seeing the board. The results are too predictable. Many of the students are not excelling. The loser kids' helmets are still behind the one-yard line, while other students' helmets are spread out over the whole field. Only a couple of helmets are approaching the end zone, and these belong to the students who were already doing well and did not need any further motivation.

Maybe this is an isolated event. Not so fast. Walk next door and witness a huge dart-board bulletin board with a paper dart for each student. The same permanent marker was used to bold each student's name on their dart. Some darts are on the bull's eye, some on outer rings and some darts are pinned up on the outside of all the rings.

Let's go to the next-door classroom.

How clever! This teacher chose a baseball diamond to motivate her students. Every student has a baseball with carefully drawn red stitching and their name in big, black, bold letters. So well-constructed. We see the names of the single-hit students, double-hit students, triple-hit students, and home-run students. Oh, and by the way, there are the strike-out students' baseballs over to the side.

I am writing about bulletin boards that I have seen personally. This is not fiction. Each time I see a fancy bulletin board like the ones mentioned above, I know what the data will show without a second glance. No matter how creative the board is, the data remain the same. There are clear winners and clear losers posted for anyone to see at any moment of the day. Sure, for some students this process works. But for most students, especially the students who have been deemed losers in their previous classes, the board may be new, but the tactic remains the same. The baseball field did not work, neither did the dart board—so what makes this football field any different? Nothing, absolutely nothing. "Ranking is a farce" (Deming, 1994, p. 25).

The Transportation Security Administration (TSA) is charged with the duty to keep airline passengers safe while they are on flights. They are responsible for assessing potential dangers and risks that passengers rarely think about as they prepare to fly. Baseball bats are not allowed in the cabin of the plane. This may seem inconvenient for baseball players who only intend to carry their bats with them on the flight. But if someone intends harm, having a baseball bat in the cabin of a plane is extremely dangerous. Used the wrong way or with the wrong motivation, a baseball bat becomes a weapon. As a frequent flier I am very glad the TSA does not allow baseball bats in the cabin of airplanes. Although most people have only joy in mind when using a baseball bat, the potential to do harm with the bat is what keeps it out of the airplane cabins.

We need DSA—Data Security Administration. Someone needs to ensure that data are not being used as a weapon in classrooms. Unfortunately, these types of charts are everywhere, from multiplication tables to books completed and behavior infractions. These charts label, humiliate, and discourage students on a day-to-day basis. Our education system is in need of adults who know how to collect the data and use them for honoring and celebrating achievements instead of comparing and embarrassing students. Data are like baseball bats; they can be used for harm or for joy.

This chapter is not intended as another cruel swipe against teachers, especially when there is already far too much negativity directed toward them. The teachers who created these bulletin boards were not intending to harm students. They have simply fallen prey to decades of bad habits—habits disguised as colorful arrangements of paper stapled onto cork boards, with unattainable goals to inspire generations of students. The goal of learning to further the human experience and improve our world has been replaced by a never-ending campaign to raise test scores. Far too often the worth of a teacher is determined by what the test data report. School funding, teacher salaries, and curriculum effectiveness all depend on what the data report and how they are interpreted.

What if the data are doing more harm than good? Data can be used for harm or joy; the way they are being used in our current education system is mostly bad. One could say atrocious. In the chapters to come I will describe how data can be used not only to maintain the kindergarten level of motivation, but to create an accurate picture of knowledge attained in the classroom, and even in the entire school.

Chapters 13 and 14 describe in great detail how numerous teachers and their principals are using data successfully. They learned the secret for captivating joy in learning and using data appropriately to illustrate that joy. No longer do their students cringe when a bulletin board shows up in their classroom, not because they are all at the touchdown line, but because these bulletin boards celebrate their achievements without causing embarrassment. Every student is honored without any hint of ranking. Data collection, for public display, is a team effort and a team celebration. These educators put the Data Security Administration (DSA) out of business and ensure that data is no longer used for harm, but for joy.

CHAPTER 8

"If You Behave after Lunch, I'll Let You Have Another Quiz"

*Our schools must preserve and nurture the yearning
for learning that everyone is born with.
Joy in learning comes not so much from what is learned,
but from the learning.*

W. Edwards Deming

Just before lunchtime, a student in Rachel Lutterman's Grade 5 class in Ruidoso, New Mexico asked, "Can we have another quiz?" Rachel answered, "If you behave after lunch, I'll let you have another quiz." This was her somewhat sarcastic way of saying, "Yes." She knew they would behave after lunch because of her expert classroom-leadership skills and positive student-teacher relationships. She knew their intrinsic motivation was being preserved and they were having fun. She understood what Deming wrote: "We must preserve the power of intrinsic motivation, dignity, cooperation, curiosity, joy in learning, that people are born with" (Deming, 1994, p. 121). Mrs. Lutterman did not rely on meaningless incentives to entice her students into wanting to learn. She did not dangle trinkets or stickers over their heads to get them to participate in her classroom discussions. Instead she tried a different strategy. And it paid off, big time.

When have you ever heard students ask for another quiz? Probably never. Part III will demonstrate the methods that Mrs. Lutterman uses effectively in her classroom to garner these results, but for now we will examine the harm caused by incentives and bribes. If teachers admit to their students that they know students will not complete academic work without a bribe, we are in trouble. Big trouble. "The less we use external, or extrinsic, rewards on our children, the more they will engage in their education for the sake and love of learning" (Lahey, 2015, p. 22).

Using the same sand and same rock from Jesus' parable, we could also say incentives signify the sand, and intrinsic signifies education built upon a rock. If the house symbolizes the process of learning and it rests on sand, no matter what technology we invent, the house will crumble. We want and need students to give 100% effort and receive great joy from the learning. The rock is the intrinsic motivation students bring with them to kindergarten; our job is to protect this rock and not allow it to be ground into the sand of incentives.

In my workshops and keynotes I often ask people to agree in a small group how many incentives students receive per day in their school. The most common agreement is five per day, but it can range anywhere from two to 20 per day. Assume a group agreed that students receive five incentives per day. Five multiplied by 180 school days in a year, multiplied by 13 years, totals 11,700 incentives over one academic career. Even though students receive over 10,000 incentives, we know that simultaneously students are losing their love of school at astronomical rates. The end result is only 5-8% of high school seniors invest in school because they love to learn. If incentives worked, this book would be unnecessary.

A teacher approached me during a break in a workshop and shared a family story. In November she and her husband had asked their teenage daughter and son what they had received 11 months earlier for the prior Christmas. Neither could remember even one gift. The parents remembered how much both children had begged and pleaded for each gift. Each child had layered reason after reason as to why they had to have *these* gifts. But 11 months later, neither child could identify even one of the Christmas gifts from the previous year. So the parents said, "There will be no gifts this Christmas; we are going to spend the money on a vacation you will never forget." It worked. The trip was a success. This family now invests their money into memorable experiences, instead of trivial trinkets that are quickly forgotten.

The same is true for the incentives used in our schools. Between the stickers, bulletin-board recognition, paper certificates, assemblies, pizza parties, extra recesses, and anything else teachers are trying, students are not becoming better learners and are not enjoying the learning process. They do not even remember most of the 11,700 incentives that have been tossed their way. They cram enough into their memory to get them to the next reward and then forget that information along with the incentives they received. For the very few students who actually remember some of the incentives they did receive, most admit that the only reason they did their work was to get the reward, not to get the knowledge. We are missing the mark big time.

Not only do students not remember our incentives, but incentives create an urge to defy, as recorded by Deci and Faste: "Self-motivation, rather than external motivation, is at the heart of creativity, responsibility, healthy behavior, and lasting change. External cunning or pressure can sometimes bring about compliance, but with compliance comes various negative consequences, including the urge to defy" (Deci and Flaste, 1995, p. 9). This defiance sometimes resembles quiet rebellion and other times looks like deliberate disobedience. It can look like a student quietly drawing an ugly picture of the teacher, but far more often it manifests as visible, auditory classroom disruption. This results in a frustrated teacher and a student labeled "behavior problem" for the rest of their educational career. However, if students are given the opportunity to learn subjects that intrigue them and touch on the very core of who they are, intrinsic motivation drives them to seek deeper into that knowledge. The energy placed into defiance is now turned into determination, and a determined student does not need an incentive to complete tasks.

Incentives do not encourage self-motivation. They are simply a bribe to complete a task.

Once the task is completed and the incentive is received, both parties (the briber and the recipient) move on without forming a meaningful attachment to the process or the material. Our students are not developing the skill of self-motivation. They require more and more incentives to do menial tasks and have less appreciation for the value of hard work.

It is well documented that incentives work only in the short term.

Teachers are left with the pressure of trying to entice students with fancier trinkets or more impressive reward systems. We want students to learn for their own well-being and success. Our world needs motivated world changers instead of languid adults who take their education for granted.

It is well-documented that incentives work only in the short term. "Try to encourage a kid to learn math by paying her for each workbook page she completes—and she'll almost certainly become diligent in the short term and lose interest in math in the long term" (Pink, 2009, 39). Incentives do not encourage students to build determination, persistence, grit, or a work ethic. In the long term, students are entering into higher education and the work force lacking these valuable attributes. "These children of praise have now entered the workforce, and sure enough, many can't function without getting a sticker for their every move" (Dweck, 2006, p. 136). This increased need for praise and incentives is exhausting employers and failing our future generations. Who knew so much was riding on the way our students learn in school?

People bring three assets of themselves into situations: their personality, their power, and their knowledge. In education, teachers have on their first day on the job 20–30 direct reports. Sometimes society seems to downplay this responsibility because the students are young. I don't. It is tough. Beginning teachers start their profession thinking their personality will solve most student issues. Personality rarely wins all students over. Some students will bond instantly with the teacher, other students will build walls around themselves and count down the days until summer. Novice teachers think, "Now what?" Two other assets are available—power and knowledge. Well, beginning teachers don't have the knowledge yet to lead so many learners, so power is their last option. Bribes are the power tool most often selected by teachers. Bribes are familiar from their own educational experience. They experienced being bribed as students and watched the teachers bribe their students during their student teaching training. Bribery is an easy tool and a quick fix, but it is not the correct tool for the job. We need to invest in building knowledge in our teachers so that they are prepared to lead their classrooms. One aim of *How to Create a Perfect School* is to greatly increase knowledge in educators. I want teachers to have the expertise to always put knowledge first because: "Rewards can perform a weird sort of behavioral alchemy: they can transform an interesting task into a drudge. They can turn play into work. And by diminishing intrinsic motivation, they can send performance, creativity, and even upstanding behavior toppling like dominoes" (Pink, 2009, p. 37).

We need to reorder the use of these three assets teachers bring into their classrooms.

Knowledge first, personality second, and then power on rare occasions. With knowledge, many teachers, like Rachel Lutterman, can preserve intrinsic motivation as her students hunger for new All-Time Bests by building new concepts upon existing knowledge. The last thing we want are experienced teachers continuing to rely upon power as their primary tool.

CHAPTER 9

"You Mean We Have to Know This, Like Forever?!"

*We want our schools to be more effective with
more students than ever before.*

Anthony Bryk

The valedictorian sauntered up to the podium as the applause thundered. His family, friends, teachers, and principal eagerly waited for him to share how he got to this place in his life. During 13 years of school he had outperformed all of his peers to win his spot at the microphone and bragging rights for his college application. He cleared his throat and leaned into the microphone.

"I am not the smartest student in this high school. I'm not the best at studying, and I can't remember what I learned three years ago when I first started at this school. To be honest, I can't even tell you what was on our finals last month. I can tell you that I am the very best student in this school at cramming. I know how to cram, receive my A, and dump all of the information out of my brain in order to make room to cram for the next test. I am not the smartest here; I am just the best at cramming."

No educator wants to hear that speech. No educator wants to admit that they already know this is happening in their classroom. I have personally sat through approximately 1000 teacher interviews in my career. During these interviews, I never heard a candidate say they wanted to become a teacher to help students learn how to cram and forget. They never mentioned they wanted to pass students along to the next teacher unprepared and unmotivated. Not once. These teacher candidates express how much they love watching the "light bulb" flip on in students' heads when they finally understood a difficult concept. They had a passion for helping students learn, remember, and easily recall information; however, the system they interviewed for is not for recall and remembering.

It was in November several years ago that a Grade 1 teacher from Kentucky heard me speak about the LtoJ process. This process removes cramming from classrooms and

> **First grade marks the initiation into the "Cram it and forget it" club.**

replaces it with a more effective learning method. Students are taught how to transfer knowledge into their long-term memory and recall it frequently. By December, the teacher had changed her spelling process. Previously, students in her class were assigned weekly spelling words on Monday, glanced at the words occasionally throughout the week, crammed on Thursday night in order to spell the words correctly on Friday, and by Saturday they had forgotten the words. When asked about the previous week's spelling words, her students would stare at her blankly. When the LtoJ method was introduced, one of her students exclaimed, "You mean we have to know how to spell these words, like forever?!" The answer was yes. However, they did not know how to learn in terms of forever. Like their teacher, they needed to learn how to make their knowledge stick, forever.

Jack Canfield wrote, "If you give your mind a $1 million dollar problem, then it will come up with a $1 million dollar solution" (Canfield, 2015, p. 109). Okay. Let's try this problem on for size: In my survey of over 3,000 teachers I asked, "What percentage of the year do you spend teaching students content they should already know?" The average was 33% of the time. Here are some round numbers for us to ponder: If the United States invests one-half of a trillion dollars in K–12 education every year—and let's say that only 25% of the time is spent teaching students content they should already know—the US is spending $125 billion a year on review. Can we get rid of permission-to-forget and our cramming-for-grades system? What you are about to read is a $125 billion solution.

First grade marks the initiation into the "Cram it and forget it" club. These young scholars do not enter school knowing this club exists, but after a few weeks of experiencing spelling tests, first graders figure out they are not going to be retested on these words, so they do not have to store them long term. No teacher tells their students they only need to know the words for Friday and then they can forget them. However, children are smart, and in about a month they have the process down pat. That is why the Grade 1 student in Kentucky was so astonished. He had learned how to cram in September and now in December he was flabbergasted by the change. "No number of successes in short-term problems will ensure long-term success" (Deming, 1994, p. 25).

By this point you may be thinking, "Well, Lee, I can see your point, but I send my child to a private school. Things are different there." Not so fast. The school may be different, the cost may be high, but the methods are similar. Not only does research indicate this, but a personal example also comes to mind.

My wife and I were visiting college friends who happened to have their grandchildren visiting at the same time. The children attended a private, Protestant Christian school.

About halfway through our visit, our friend asked their granddaughter to sing for us. She quickly agreed. As she was standing before us ready to sing, her Grandma asked her to share the Bible verses she had recently learned at school. Her granddaughter replied, "I don't remember that; it was just for a test." Grandma looked at me and said, "Well, Lee, that's what you have been saying: all that time and money, and she doesn't remember a few Bible verses."

The singing was beautiful. Not a word or note forgotten. The memory verses, however, were forgotten just like the spelling words from the earlier example. Singing interested the young girl and drove her to know and understand the music. The memory verses did not have the same effect. The same methods of cram and forget are still encouraged in the private schools, and the results are exactly the same as in public schools.

Approximately 80% of my work is in public schools, 10% in charter schools, and 10% in Christian (both Catholic and Protestant) schools. I state this because students have permission to forget in all types of educational experiences. The cram/forget habit is everywhere shared by everyone. The following quotations by education professionals illustrate this truth.

"In high school students ask, 'Do we have to know this for the test?' What they are asking for is permission to forget" (Thompson, 1995, p. 67).

"If academically-oriented experiences are not stored in permanent memory, they are not added to academic background knowledge" (Marzano, 2004, p. 21).

"Too many children and adolescents experience vocabulary instruction as making passing acquaintances with a wide range of words. They know that many of the words won't be used again, and that next week there will be a new list" (Fisher, Frey, and Hattie, 2016, p. 49).

"It seems that when people learn with the expectation of being evaluated, they focus on memorizing facts, but they don't process the information as fully, so they don't grasp the concepts as well . . . those who had learned expecting to be tested had forgotten much more . . . Evidently, they memorized the material for the test, and when the test was over, they pulled the plug and let it drain out" (Deci, 1995, p. 48).

Fisher, Frey, Hattie, Marzano, Thompson, and Deci comment on this problem without specifying that the problem is nationwide. They do not have to make this specification because the problem is all too common. How can we ever have more effective schools if we continue to insist that the cram-and-forget method is the best or only method and ignore that it is not producing favorable results? The answer is you cannot have more effective schools using this method. Cramming and dumping knowledge is not an effective method for learning.

Maybe there are some students who love cramming, knowing full well they will soon forget the crammed content. I have yet to meet them. On our Will & Thrill Matrix the highest feedback a student can score is a 5 for 100% effort at cramming, but hating the fake learning process. A 5 is mediocre and our students deserve more than mediocre.

University professors often complain about the lack of knowledge possessed by their incoming freshmen. The high-school teachers complain about the lack of knowledge of their incoming freshmen. The middle-school teachers complain about the lack of knowledge of their Grade 6 students. The intermediate teachers in Grades 3, 4, and 5 complain about the lack of knowledge coming into Grade 3. That is a lot of complaining and very little being done about the fact that very few of our students are adequately learning regardless of who is to blame.

The university professors use the same cram/forget process as high-school teachers. The high-school teachers use the same cram/forget process as the middle-school teachers. The middle-school teachers use the same cram/forget process as the elementary teachers in Grades 1–5.

Somehow, someway, we need to stop the blame game and realize all levels of education are victims of the same sequence of cram/get-a-grade/forget mentality. It is possible to change these patterns if educators take the time to learn new habits. Habits that not only empower our teachers, but engage our students and produce incredible results: habits that lead to nearly six times higher learning retention and produce students eager to learn and remember. It is not a far-off dream. It can be very much a reality when the methods used in the LtoJ process are implemented and the cram-and-forget method is left caged in the past.

CHAPTER 10

What Percentage of Our Students Feel Dumb?

Nobody ever gets used to feeling dumb.

Carol Dweck

In my first book on the education system, *Improving Student Learning: Applying Deming's Principles in Classrooms*, I quoted a grandfather who attended a Springfield, Missouri elementary school awards assembly. Here is what he wrote to the editor:

This morning I took time off from work to attend the first-grade awards ceremony at my grandson's school. I did this because I am a good grandparent and because I feel some responsibility as a fellow teacher to support colleagues. Of some 100 shiny-faced, freshly scrubbed soon-to-be-second graders, the same 15 students were invited onstage time and time again to receive awards in art, spelling, physical education, reading, and so on. After the awards were presented in each area, the small group of winning students lined up in front of the stage to face the audience and bask briefly in the cheers and applause.

By the end of the presentation, I had seen those children and heard their names so often I felt as though I knew them.

After the awards were given out, all the remaining first-graders were marched briskly across the stage to accept their completion certificates and return to their seats with no time for any recognition from the audience. This was done without fanfare. The lady next to me said of her daughter, 'They are breaking her heart.' The man on the other side replied, 'We send them here to learn so early that they are not valuable.'

Next year, I will take my grandson fishing on awards day. His teacher may say, 'That family just doesn't care,' or 'No wonder he is not doing any better.' "We do care. I just don't want to watch him hurt again. (B. Thomas quoted in Jenkins, 2003)

The grandfather in the above story makes a key statement: "We do care. I just don't want to watch him get hurt again." Even in first grade, students are painfully aware of who the winners are and who are the losers in their class. They know if they measure up because it is reinforced again and again. If they measure up, they get the awards, move their name across the bulletin board and receive praise. But if they do not measure up, they conclude they must be dumb. Once this feeling of being dumb is reinforced multiple times, the discouragement sets in and the student will resent learning and school. "Nobody ever gets used to feeling dumb" (Dweck, p. 219).

For whatever reason, we believe that the students who do not receive recognition are actually happy for the students who do receive the accolades. There is an unspoken desire to use the students who are winning as living inspiration for the students who are falling short. We hope that by publicly acknowledging the students who achieve greatness, we will encourage other students to try harder to also become winners. When we write that logic out, it sounds pretty stupid, doesn't it?

Every time I hear the word *stupid* I cannot help but remember an event several years ago when my three-year-old grandson informed us that he needed to go potty. So, being the helpful grandpa that I am, I volunteered. Unfortunately, there was not a urinal in the restroom. No problem. I put the toilet seat back against the tank and lifted up grandson to relieve himself. All was going according to plan until the toilet seat fell down and hit grandson on the head. While consoling a crying, peeing grandson, I said, "That stupid toilet seat!" We finished our business, dried his tears, and returned my grandson to his parents.

It was then that my grandson exclaimed, "Grandpa said a bad word." My wife Sandy looked at me and in a sweet but firm tone said, "Lee, what did you say?" I looked bewildered and innocent.

> "No child can feel safe and feel like a failure at the same time."

Then my grandson enthusiastically continued to tattle on me: "Grandpa said, 'stupid.'" It was then that daughter-in-law explained that they were trying to get their son to stop saying 'stupid' about everything. My wife and I relaxed and had a good laugh about everything except maybe the sore head.

What could be more stupid than thinking we can publicly honor the high-achievement students in front of the less academic students and think schools will improve from this effort? I started this chapter with the title, "What percentage of students think they are dumb?" My research suggests that approximately 40% of students in high school think they are dumb. Everything we do to create more students who think they are dumb is stupid. To make it even worse, when children have been traumatized, they not only feel dumb, they do not feel safe. Janyne McConnaughey, author of *Brave, a Personal Story of Healing Childhood Trauma*, and my sister, wrote to me in an email, "No child can feel safe and feel like a failure at the same time." She continued, "So, is intrinsic motivation lost when children do not feel safe? I think so. It goes back to my research on the view of the child. Teachers who do not trust children to learn must be in control—of everything. Control is deadly to traumatized children who were controlled in unsafe relationships."

I have heard critics contesting the opinion I just wrote. They argue that children need to learn how to lose. We need competition; that is what made America great. I hope my responses sticks in the minds of readers for the rest of their lives.

    A. Children do need to learn about competition. They learn this best in games and sports. We want children to learn how to be good losers and how to be good winners. In a game of Yahtzee with four players, we have three losers and one winner. The loss is not damaging to the self-concept. In athletic games between teams seldom do we have a tie; one team wins and one team loses. The pain is minimal and can soon be replaced with a win during the next competition.

In reference to academic losses, the pain exists for a lifetime. Students spend on average six hours a day, five days a week, for 10 months of the year in school. That is an overwhelmingly large amount of time to be publicly confronted with your weaknesses. Academic loss damages self-confidence, diminishes the wonder of learning, stifles individual strengths and redefines a student's self-worth. This is far more detrimental than losing a game of Yahtzee once in a while.

B.   We can have only winners in academic learning. No parent sends their children to school to be a loser. How can all children be winners? Because, in the words of John Maxwell, we want kids to think, "I only want to be better than my former self." Principal Diane Benito wrote, "Students are able to visually see this growth by becoming involved with the graphing. I love how it changes their mindset from *how many I got wrong* to, *I know more than I have ever known before!*"

In case readers are tempted to think what I have written is unique to the United States of America, one can read "How the Education System Is Making Kids Stressed and Sick" by Hayley Gleeson from Australia. She quotes extensively from author Lucy Clark, who writes, "All types of assessment and judgment paralysed her (my daughter) with anxiety. She wanted to flee classes, she truanted, and suspension and expulsion were always around the corner. Getting her to school was a daily struggle. I realised that we weren't the only family in pain when I wrote an article about her finally finishing school—and what an incredible achievement that was for her—and the feedback I got from around the world made me realise how many kids feel like this." (https://www.abc.net.au/news/2016-07-17/beautiful-failures-education-making-kids-sick/7589084).

Clark continues, "I don't think it is up to kids to work out how to cope better with the pressure. It is up to the adults in their lives—their parents, their teachers, and the leaders of their society—all of us—to work out ways to reduce that pressure and to seriously question what the pressure is for." Why there is so much pressure is a great question. Basically, it is because of poor psychology. We have come to believe that students are naturally unmotivated and adults need to pressure and motivate them. The truth is they come to school already motivated and the responsibility of adults is to maintain this motivation.

In an environment where students (1) are continually recognized for personally doing better than ever before and (2) know they contributed to the success of the team, students learn cooperation. In an environment where adults are mature, children learn to enjoy the games whether they win or lose. In both games and academic environments we want students to give great effort and to receive great joy because they are enjoying the process, not seeking empty glory.

CHAPTER 11

Homework is NOT a School Subject

Attention needs to move from how to teach to how to learn.

John Hattie

Homework is a commonly used method for helping students learn. At times homework is a positive tool; often it is a negative one. Some families love homework and others resent teachers telling them how to spend their family time in the evenings. Sometimes homework is merely busy work hastily assigned at the last minute because of a board policy on homework.

Sometimes it prepares students very well for an upcoming Advanced Placement exam. Whatever the reason, feeling, or policy regarding homework, we must agree that homework is not a school subject and does not guarantee academic success.

Homework can take many different forms. Reading assignments, group or individual projects, book reports, research papers, test preparation, and chapter questions all fall into the category of "homework." In this chapter, we will be referring mainly to the daily assignments that are sent home with one day to complete as homework.

In my years of interviewing teacher candidates, the answer, "I want to be a homework monitor," was never given in response to the question, "Why do you want to be a teacher?" Sadly, far too many professionals with the official title of "teacher" are becoming homework monitors. A majority of the instructional time in too many middle- and high-school classrooms is consumed trading papers for scoring, arguing about correctness of certain answers, and teaching the content missed by a few students. Other teachers spend hours upon unpaid hours grading homework instead of investing time preparing engaging experiences for actual course content. The enthusiasm teachers begin their career with is quickly sucked away with the nightly chore of scoring papers. This reality, paired with the very high percentage of homework that students simply copy from their classmates, is truly a waste of energy, talent, and time.

What do teachers desire? They want the content of their course to be placed in students' long-term memory. They want the surface-learning to be instantly recalled when needed for deep-learning problems, and they want their students to be able to transfer both surface and deep-learning to new situations inside and outside of school. None of these goals are effectively accomplished when homework overpowers course content and subject exploration.

I have purposely ended each part of this book with a chapter for parents. Teachers really do need parents on their side. Grading practices are a major deterrent to this partnership.

Complicated scoring systems, intricate requirements, and nonsense assignments leave parents confused when they are trying to understand their child's homework. When a student receives 20 zeros on homework assignments along with four As on exams, the result is a C at best. How does any student keep their Will and Thrill for learning when they prove on the exams they learned the content in spite of their refusal to use the approved method (homework) to learn? Couple this with the fact that a majority of the secondary students who receive credit for turning in homework copied it from a classmate and you can imagine why parents struggle with supporting homework. Homework does not indicate a child's level of intelligence, just their level of obedience.

Many parents determine if a teacher or school is acceptable based on the amount of homework assigned. When teachers choose not to assign homework, you can bet there is pushback from parents. After all, that is what they did when they were in school. This misinformed view of homework deceives parents into thinking that the daily work their student brings home is an effective learning tool. In actuality, assigning more or less homework has little to do with student learning and knowledge retention. It may even lead to lower academic performance because it often crushes student Will and Thrill, exactly what we're trying to stop from happening.

In Chapter 4 I shared a way to gain accurate data from students. The same method can be used to answer questions about how students feel about the effectiveness of homework. Ask students to write down the names of 10 friends and tell them you are going to ask them questions about homework. Let them know that you will *NOT* be collecting the names of the students; you only interested in knowing numbers.

> A. How many of your 10 friends copy daily homework?
>
> B. How many of your friends say they learn a lot from homework?
>
> C. How many of your friends think daily homework is only busywork—that it is not helpful?
>
> D. How many of your friends think homework should be a part of their overall grade?

Our students and parents must understand that the goal is for students to learn; the method is far less important than learning. Further, we desire for students to exhibit effort and joy in the learning process. Once the data from your social survey is collected, create a quick graph on the whiteboard showing the number of Fs, Ds, Cs, Bs, and As on the last exam.

Allow the students to agree on a method, other than homework, to decrease the Ds and Fs and increase the Bs and As. Allow students to establish a hypothesis to test. If the tested hypothesis does not result in improved learning, call another class meeting to establish a new hypothesis.

For some students, homework may be a necessity. For others, it may only be busywork. The key is to find which methods work for each student.

Homework is a symptom of an underlying problem. The underlying problem focuses more on the method

> ...the goal is for students to learn; the method is far less important than learning.

than the learning. There is no method ever invented that works for 100% of the students. None. Not all kids learn from the new high-tech, five-million-dollar software system. Not all kids learn to read with phonics. Not all kids learn with educational games. Not all students learn from the handwritten comments on their papers. And not all learn from homework.

My dream consists of a learning environment where students give us 100% effort and receive great joy along the way. When this is accomplished, students arrive at class motivated to absorb the material and actively participate in their learning. When Will and Thrill are in place, student learning will exceed expectations. Educators should not relax on standards for learning, but should relax on methods. Who really cares by what method the students place the content in their long-term memory?

* I know readers may doubt the word "majority" when I talked about students copying homework. I encourage you to do your own research, asking high-school relatives and family friends. Do not ask these students if they copy homework; instead ask, "In a class of 20–25 students how many of them copy homework instead of doing it themselves?")

CHAPTER 12

Imperfect for Parents

We conclude that until there is a consensus on student performance among educators and parents, individual schools will find it extremely difficult to improve the quality of instruction.

W. Edwards Deming

As the third monthly kindergarten meeting began, Mrs. Anderson waited for the parents' chatter to quiet down. She cleared her throat and began, "The responsibility of unions is to represent the people who pay their dues. Police unions represent police, pilot unions represent pilots, and teacher unions represent teachers. Students do not have unions; they have parents.

"All parents have a responsibility to represent their children, but how they choose to represent and advocate for their children can differ greatly. At one end of the spectrum are parents who always take the side of their child—no matter what the situation. Even further they are available daily to solve every minor problem, quickly absorbing any consequences or responsibilities away from the child. In the United States of America we call these types of parents 'helicopter parents' because they are always hovering over the child. In Scandinavian countries they are called sweeper parents after the sport of curling—always sweeping away any and all irritations the child might encounter.

"On the other end of the spectrum are the parents who believe the school personnel are always right. They tell their children to just deal with the problem. Lee Jenkins tells the story of his father, who camped out toward the end of this spectrum. This wasn't always true, but he was more likely to side with the school professionals rather than being a helicopter parent to his children.

"If Lee came home from school complaining that he was punished unjustly for something, his father asked him if he could think of anything he did wrong the past couple weeks for which he did not get caught. Lee could always answer, 'Well, yes, I guess so.' His father would then respond, 'Well, just take the punishment for the wrongdoing you didn't get caught for.' Lee still remembers years later how much he hated that sequence of questions and answers. Educators know that we are not always right and proving we are right is not our goal. We need you to advocate for your children in the important matters because with over 20 students in each classroom, we know we miss things. We want to partner with you on your child's educational journey.

"Finally, there are the parents who need a wake-up call from thinking his or her child is always right. There is the story about a student sent to the principal's office for breaking a rule. She admitted to the principal that she broke the rules. So, the principal informed the student that he would be calling her mom. The student strongly reminded the principal how much her mom hated being called at work, saying, 'Go ahead and call my mom. I will deny I broke the rules. My mom always believes me.'

"Without missing a beat, the principal nodded and excused the student from his office for a moment. He proceeded to call her mom at work and tell her that he was bringing her daughter into the office. The phone would be on speaker phone without her daughter's knowledge. He asked her to be silent and to just listen to the conversation. Once the mother agreed, he called the student back into his office and continued their conversation.

Principal: Now, where did we leave off? Oh, I remember you admitted you stole a dollar out of a student's backpack.

Daughter: Yes, that's right. I took the dollar.

Principal: Then I told you I need to call your mother.

Daughter: I told you how much my mother hates being called at work. Besides, I will tell her I didn't take the dollar. She always believes me.

Mom: (A voice booming out of the speaker phone) Young lady, meet me at the curb by the fire hydrant in front of the school! I will be there in five minutes!!

"So, parents, what criteria can we use to navigate the tricky space between the parent/child are always right and the teacher/school are always right? Understand that I am not talking about serious issues that need to be investigated. I am talking about the normal ups and downs that naturally occur with 500 people inside the same space. These issues include minor behavior infractions, disagreements with peers or teachers, and other character-building opportunities.

"Sometimes it is hard to know when to intervene and when to let our students learn from their challenges. Here is how I determine whether or not I should intervene when I receive concerns from students or parents: First I ask myself if the stated problem is unique to an individual or has applications to many more, if not all students. Very often parents see issues of which I am not aware. These practices may have the potential to harm many students, not only the particular student in question. If the problem is unique to a particular student, then I will think of unique, personal solutions versus school-wide discussions.

"My hope, parents, is that you let your children deal with most of the bumps and bruises of schooling. School provides an opportunity for children to work through social/emotional challenges. It encourages them to become confident problem solvers and independent thinkers. They will fail a lot, but those failures will lead to great joy when they do succeed. Please do not rob your child of this great joy by solving all of their problems in order to protect them from failing. Do let us know if a major problem arises and we will partner with you to create solutions.

"Beyond that, what I most hope for is that we work together to fix the system that causes most students to lose their interest in school learning. That is the major issue that affects every student. Regardless of the type of representation that you lean toward for your student, please find a healthy balance between *your student is always right* and *the system is always right*. Neither of these statements are 100% true. Both are capable of failure which is why we need a well-structured middle ground when representing our students.

"In our upcoming monthly meetings, I will outline the practices that have been around for generations that are responsible for much of the decline of intrinsic motivation in students. Then on a visit to a classroom I will share with you firsthand what our teachers are doing to eliminate these problems. You will have the opportunity to observe the power of intrinsic motivation in action. We are making great strides towards changing the education system and I am excited for you each to see what we are doing in our classrooms.

"In the future, if you find that your child is struggling or that their motivation seems to be dwindling, please reach out and talk to us. Our hope is to provide you with guidance in order to create an educational system that works for all students, not just a handful of students. We are fighting against decades of bad practices, which means that it is going to take some time and a lot of communication. We need to hear from you when things are working and when things are not working. We cannot fix what is not working if we do not know about it.

"Lee Jenkins shares another story about a summer day when he was a school superintendent. This is an example of a problem unique to an individual student. A parent called about her formerly eager-to-learn son who now hated school. Through tears, she shared that her son was very bright, but something was drastically wrong.

"As Lee listened to the distraught mother explain the history of her son's loss of effort and joy, he became convinced that she was correct. Something was wrong. It came to light, in the words of her son, 'I will be starting Grade 5 in September, but I should be going into Grade 6.' Her son had been retained in Grade 1 and had become painfully aware that he was not with his friends or peer group. He was reminded every day that back in Grade 1 he had not made the cut. Dr. Jenkins suggested the student skip Grade 5 and be restored to his age grouping.

"Seven years later, Lee received a thank-you letter from that same mother, sharing that her son recently graduated high school. From the day he entered Grade 6 with his original peer group, he was a different child. She was convinced that if they had not reversed the Grade 1 retention he never would have graduated. She saw her son's passion for learning return and was so grateful she chose to speak up.

"I tell this story because it was the parent's attitude that set the stage for an unusual solution. The parent did not blame any of the people in the school district. She merely informed Lee that there was a problem, and asked if he could offer any help in this situation. It was the teamwork between the mother, the superintendent, and the child that created the solution. No blaming necessary. This is my hope for us. We can bring about change, using teamwork and creative problem solving to ensure that all of our students enter and leave school excited to learn.

"John Maxwell's attitude is what I want to embrace with all of you. He wrote, 'When I'm leading people through a difficult situation, I often don't know all of the answers. But I do know there are answers, and I'll do everything I can to make sure we find out what they are' (Maxwell, 2014, p. 134).

"Thank you for spending part of your morning with me. On your way out is a document outlining four of the normal methods used in education that douse the flame of intrinsic motivation in students. These procedures include: keeping the year-long learning expectations a secret, using charts that publicly embarrass students, encouraging students to cram and forget, and placing too much of a focus on one method to learn (homework, for example) over the actual learning of the year-long content. As you read, I hope to spark your curiosity. I hope it will help you to truly appreciate the replacements you will see when we tour classrooms during our next monthly meeting. I am excited to hear your input and to show off all that your students are accomplishing using these new approaches. See you next month."

Replacements for Imperfect Processes that Decimate the Perfect Dream

It takes a lot of work to make something so complex look so easy.

Bryan Kramer

Every chapter in Part III of *How to Create a Perfect School* will seem crazy and impossible to achieve. Your first thoughts will probably be:

1. Students will be overwhelmed by the BIGGIE.
2. Students do not care about working hard on a non-graded quiz.
3. There is not enough time to give these quizzes and create all of these graphs.

Carol Dweck's powerful writing in *Growth Mindset* clearly describes the stark difference between a fixed mindset and a growth mindset. Part II of *How to Create a Perfect School* describes some of the fixed-mindset habits that have harmed students worldwide for decades. In order for schools to change from this fixed-mindset structure to a growth-mindset system some "crazy" changes are necessary. Part III is about the "crazy."

Nothing fuels effort and joy more than ATBs, the daily evidence of growth!

Educators and parents will not be using the term "growth mindset;" they will be celebrating All-Time Bests. The loud ring of ATBs will reverberate off the walls of both home and school. Nothing fuels effort and joy more than ATBs, the daily evidence of growth!

CHAPTER 13

Trillions of Dollars Later and Education is Still Missing the Biggie!

"Learning can be defined as the process of developing sufficient surface knowledge to then move to deeper understanding such that one can appropriately transfer this learning to new tasks and situations"

Doug Fisher, Nancy Frey, John Hattie

While conducting a seminar on Kwajalein Island, I used an activity described by Bob Pike in his book, *Master Trainer Handbook*. Over the course of the three days I explained seven items that are essential for classroom implementation. The items were run charts, scatter diagrams, histograms, item analyses, key-concept lists, perfect feedback forms and the Will & Thrill Matrix. After I finished teaching the content, I gave the educators in the workshop Mr. Pike's assignment.

Fig. 13.1

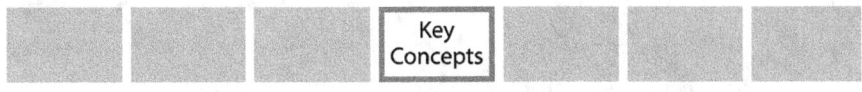

Their tasks were to write the tools I taught on seven index cards. Then they were to agree on and organize the seven index cards so that the most difficult for classroom implementation was in the middle. Next they were to decide on the two next most difficult tools to implement and place them on either side of the center one until the two easiest were at the outer edges. The best part of this activity was observing that almost every group chose the BIGGIE as the most difficult item for classroom implementation. They decided that the BIGGIE was either in the center or adjacent to the center. Writing down the essential surface-learnings concepts that students were to learn for the entire duration of a course, and then giving the list to students the first week of class, was considered to be the hardest to implement.

I agree with their decision and so do most of the participants in my other workshops.

However, there is always some initial pushback regarding telling students what they are to learn for a whole year. It is often a misguided sympathy for students—not wanting to overwhelm them. There is no reason to feel sorry when using this process. Students should know what they are expected to learn every year. Much like a driver in a new city needs a map to navigate, students need a list of key concepts to navigate their new school-year responsibilities. The destination for our students should not be kept secret and students love knowing where the teacher is going for the year. "Some actions—like installing a cash register—pay off again and again. These onetime choices require a little bit of effort up front but create increasing value over time" (Clear, 2018, p. 172). Yes, admittedly, the BIGGIE takes time, but the payoffs last for years and years.

When teachers say this is the hardest to implement, I reply, "As an educator I completely understand why this is so hard. We educators are given programs to teach, standards using an attorney-type numbering system (1.002.35.b, for example), homework policies, requirements for number of grades per week, and weekly times to go to the computer lab for state-test preparation. Almost nobody requires teachers to write down what students are to learn. Exceptions to this are most often in kindergartens and high-school vocational courses."

I then continue, saying, "People outside education are in disbelief; they cannot imagine educators do not know precisely what students are to learn for the year. They think writing down what students are to learn should be an easy first step, but this is the last thing educators think to provide for their students. When we tell students what they are going to learn for the year we become their leaders and leadership is what is far too often missing in classrooms."

Liliana Velasco has the responsibility at Columbus High School (in Nebraska) of helping new teachers learn how to implement the LtoJ process you will learn about in this section. Almost all of the new teachers she works with are in their first year of teaching. She asks her audience to look around the room at each other. After they have observed each other she says, "You all look like your students. The first day of school your students are going to look at you, then look around at their classmates and wonder why they should pay attention to someone who looks just like them. When you provide a list of essential key concepts to your students on the first day of class, your students will know that you are confident in the direction that you are leading them. If you do not do this, your students will spend the year testing you to see if you know what you are doing." This amazing advice Liliana gives these first-year teachers is leadership of learning. LOL is not only for Laughing Out Loud.

It should be noted that providing a list of essential key concepts and providing a syllabus are not the same thing. A syllabus is usually a list of topics, whereas key concepts are precise descriptions of the content to be learned. When writing the list of essential key concepts, teachers should list each concept in student-friendly language. Teachers must identify the difference between trivial knowledge and essential knowledge. They must include only what is essential for students to place in long-term memory. Trivia can and should be taught because it is often very interesting, but students are not accountable for remembering trivia. We are providing this list to help students learn and remember; it's that simple. "When students learn how to gain an overall picture of what is to be learnt, have an understanding of the success criteria for the lessons to come and are somewhat clear at the outset about what it means to master the lessons, then their subsequent learning is maximized" (Hattie and Conoghue, 2016, p. 6).

Teachers always ask for an estimate regarding how many key concepts are on the lists. There is no definitive answer, but there are examples to guide teachers. Math key concepts range from 25–50 per year, science key concepts are closer to 100, while history and geography (when combined on one list) are usually between 75 and 125. Spelling words start with about 150 words in Grade 1 and gradually increase to around 400 new words each year by the end of elementary school. World language teachers typically have 400 new vocabulary words per grade level and secondary English teachers typically place 50 to 75 additional literary terms and other vocabulary on the list each year. The number depends on grade level, curriculum, state standards, and difficulty of the curriculum. It will fluctuate, but it should always only include the essential pieces of information.

The number of key concepts need not be an even number such as 100. I actually prefer to have 98 or 103 on the list. 100 is acceptable, but maybe trivia was added to the list to reach 100 or maybe something essential was dropped from the list. These odd numbers indicate great attention was paid to the list and that nothing was added to end up with a round number.

The difference between trivial information and essential knowledge is a value judgment. There are no rules. As a guide, think, "Do I really want students to know this concept and not need to look it up on the internet?" For example, students can use the internet to determine the capital of Germany, but they should not have to use the internet to determine on which continent to find Germany.

Remember, the purpose of the key concept list is to assist student learning. It is very helpful for students when teachers continually refer to the key concept list as they teach lessons. They also help students recognize how to file away these concepts by placing subheadings inside the list. A general science teacher, for example, might place essential key concepts under headings such as astronomy, earth science, botany, and so on. "Schemata, or schemas, are the basic units by which we organize and structure our knowledge ... it is at the level of the schema that deeper meaning occurs, and the grasp on an 'overall big picture' becomes possible" (Hattie and Yates, 2014, p. 130). By breaking the list into smaller chunks or schemas, teachers set students up for success in understanding how each of the concepts build onto the next.

The next, and even harder step, is for the key concept lists to be aligned from grade level to grade level. Whatever is written on the Grade 5 science list, for example, cannot be written on any other list for any other grade level through middle or high school. Students have the right to be taught new content every year. Textbook editors organize content from former years as if it was brand new content. How boring! If one of our goals is to deny students the opportunity to forget material, then they must be taught in a manner in which they are expected to remember and use the material from previous years.

> "I had no clue you taught that; I teach it also."

During a follow-up seminar with kindergarten through twelfth-grade teachers, I asked them all to bring their current math books. The kindergarten teachers sat next to the Grade 1 teachers. They matched the units in the Grade 1 book already taught in kindergarten. Then the Grade 1 teachers provided the same insight to their Grade 2 colleagues. This continued on through high school. The teachers were in constant awe, as they had no clue what was taught in prior years unless they themselves had taught other grade levels. I have had the exact same experience with middle- and high-school science teachers. The chemistry teacher expressed to the biology teacher, "I had no clue you taught that; I teach it also." Maybe this is why teachers often ask their students, "Now, you had this last year, right?" and the students respond in unison, "No, we have not seen that before." It is not in the students' best interest to admit that they were already taught something in prior years because then they would be held accountable for remembering that information.

When teachers align content, they are in charge instead of the students or the textbook publishers. This alignment is absolutely crucial. It takes at least a full day of staff development time to align a subject from grade level to grade level. One of the very best uses of a staff development day is for administrators to set aside time for key concept alignment. Even relatively simple alignment, such as organizing spelling lists between grade levels, will take a full day. Each grade level should all have different concepts listed, and this requirement alone calls for time and space to discuss which concepts should be on which lists.

I have described the two phases for implementing the BIGGIE—(1) require teachers to provide key concepts for students, and (2) align the whole school, department, or school district so that the concepts are unique to each grade level. Some readers will be the only teacher in their school who provides the key-concept list for their students and will not be granted the opportunity to align with colleagues. These teachers can only follow the first phase; they are not the administrator who provides time for all teachers to align the key concepts.

My hope is that teachers involved with key-concept development and alignment will become advocates for the entire LtoJ process for their schools and districts. These teachers are the forerunners for improvement in their schools. Their success in the classroom will champion this improvement in beliefs and methodology to both colleagues and students.

The major objection to what I have just written is found under the umbrella of twenty-first-century learning. A quick search of the internet will bring up multiple opinions regarding what is the most important learning for students today. Much of the essence of twenty-first-century learning I hear in educator conversations is:

1. Because access to the internet is so available with computers and smart phones, there is no reason to bother with students placing surface-learning in their long-term memory.

2. Students can look up the answer to basic knowledge questions on their phones.

3. The time formerly spent on surface-learning should be spent on deep learning.

4. The advocates of twenty-first-century learning say, "No more factoids!"

Those who object to what I am writing about in regard to the key-concept lists are in the majority. While delivering a statewide keynote, I showed John Hattie's learning triangle I asked the audience members to decide which of the three levels of learning they think is the biggest current problem in US education. I directed, "Stand up if surface-learning is our biggest problem." Nobody stood up. "Now, stand up if deep-learning is the biggest problem."

Fig. 13.1

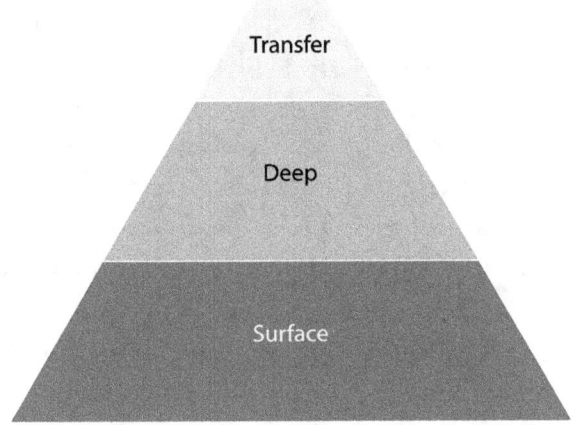

Half stood up. "Now stand up if transfer-learning is the biggest problem." The rest of the audience stood up. I then told the audience, "I am the only person in the room who thinks our biggest problem is surface-learning. Here's why: Even though the majority of the instructional time is spent on surface-learning, students do not remember it. We have all inherited a forgetting school system—not a remembering school system."

Because so much classroom time is spent on surface-learning, it is easy for many educators to be convinced that now much of this time should be spent on deep-learning. The students can search the internet for any surface-learning they need to solve

We have all inherited a forgetting school system—not a remembering school system.

deep-learning problems. The best arguments against this thinking that I have read comes from Hattie and Conoghue. "Developing 21st century skills sui generis are most misleading. These skills are often promoted as content free and are able to be developed in separate courses (e.g. critical thinking, resilience). Our model, however, suggests that such skills are likely to be best developed relative to some content" (Hattie and Conoghue, 2016, p. 9).

The reality is that remembered surface-learning is necessary for success with deep learning. "An explicit assumption is that higher level thinking requires a sufficient corpus of lower level surface knowledge to be effective—one cannot move straight to higher level thinking without sufficient level of content knowledge" (Hattie and Conoghue, p. 4). Even further, forgotten surface-learning is not transferred to other school subjects or out of school topics. "The important motive underpinning acquiring ideas and facts is that they are easily accessed when you need them in the future. Durable and accessible ideas must be laid down carefully using deliberate focus and some level of mental effort" (Hattie and Yates, 2014, p. 129).

My 20 years of experience, developing what you are reading, has proven the system can be changed so that (1) students remember surface-learning (effectiveness), (2) 25–33% less instructional time can be spent on surface-learning (efficiency), and (3) students love becoming assessment capable: completing all surface-learning data responsibilities (engagement). I know that it sounds crazy to write that students can remember much more surface-learning with less classroom time allocated to surface-learning, but it is the truth. The details follow in the rest of Part III. With the saved time and remembered surface-learning, deep-learning has a much better chance of being successful. Hattie and Yates write, "Experts were adept at shifting their students' work products over from surface to deep response requirements" (Hattie and Yates, 2014, p. 107).

For example, the key-concept item on the student-friendly list might say, "Find the volume of a right rectangular prism with fractional edge lengths. V = lwh." A follow-up deep-learning question could be, "What is the volume of the school cafeteria?" The surface-learning key concept teaches the specific skill, while the deep-learning question connects the skill to real-life applications.

One of the suggestions for increased success with deep-learning is to not have a quick due date for deep-learning assignments. Let students think about the issue for some time to solve the questions on their own. Students often think of the solution while not directly thinking about the problem. This occurs while walking, riding a bike, taking a shower, or other activities that take little thought. Readers know this is true in their personal life, and it is true for students also. I suggest the following format when students turn in their deep-learning questions:

1. Write the question

2. Write your answer

3. Describe the process you used. It is the description here that is evaluated by the teacher.

One of the best uses of scheduled time for educators to collaborate is to provide everyone in the group a copy of the same list of essential surface-learning key concepts. Then, brainstorm together a deep-learning question for each of the key concepts. These can be compiled into a document and made available for teachers to use as a part of their normal instruction. They can be used for the whole class or for only some of the students. This gives both students and teachers a simplified and specific resource that clearly states what is expected as students utilize their surface-learning knowledge to expand into success with deep-learning.

When I surveyed over 3,000 teachers with the question, "What percentage of the year do you spend teaching students content they should already know?" the average of all the answers was 33%. In order to greatly reduce this wasted time and spend it on deep-learning, change in the normal habits of schooling is essential. It all starts with the BIG-

GIE. "The more knowledge you have the easier it is to learn even more" (Hattie and Yates, p. 122). I would like to add to their quotation, "The more knowledge you forget, the harder it is to learn even more."

CHAPTER 14

The All-Time Best Distribution Center

I only want to be better than my former self.

John Maxwell

If you walk into Miranda LeBrie's classroom in Fremont, Nebraska, you will see a pair of desks with the label, "All-Time Best Distribution Center." Two of her fourth-grade students are in charge of distributing the sticker and cut-out shape to each student who earned an ATB. This simple and genius process reinforces a visible and engaging weekly event: everyone's goal is to outperform their prior individual best. After each quiz on a random sample of the surface-learning key concepts described in Chapter 13, students are honored for improving. Two extremely powerful feelings are "appreciation and gratitude" (Canfield, 2015, p. 73). The simple appreciation and gratitude students receive from their teacher and peers for earning an All-Time Best is indeed powerful. It is very simple: "Did I do better than I have ever done before?" and if so, I am shown appreciation and gratitude at the ATB Distribution Center. "When data is used correctly to enhance experience, trust goes up" (Kramer, 2016, p. 31). Kramer's insight is equally true for adults and for students.

As you read Chapter 14 you will learn the steps in leading of learning for each individual student. There is a big difference between teaching, practicing, testing, and the leading of learning. Students know the difference between being pushed and being led. Extrinsic motivation is used to push students to learn whereas when students have maintained their

Fig. 14.1

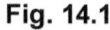

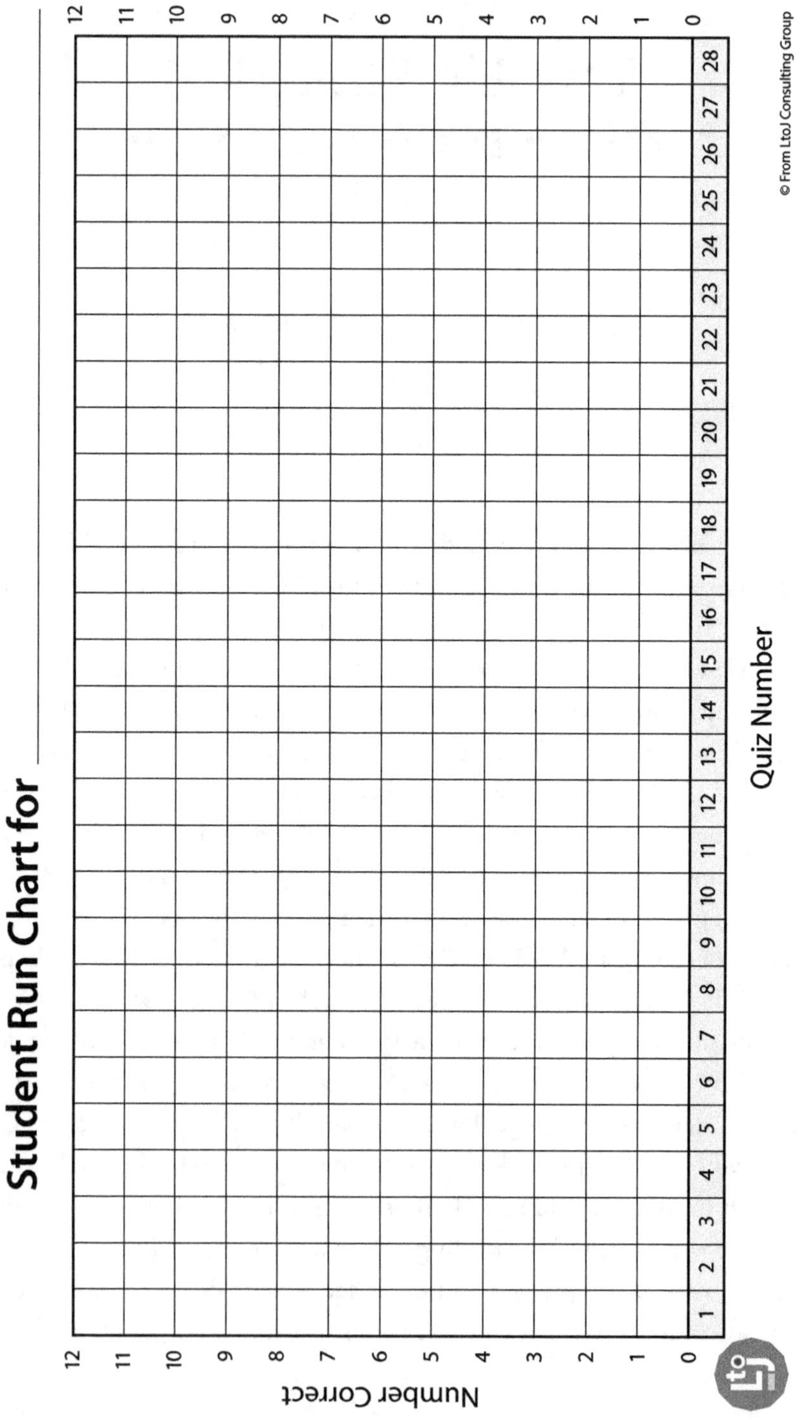

Student Run Chart for
Number Correct
Quiz Number
© From LtoJ Consulting Group

kindergarten level of intrinsic motivation, they desire for the teacher to lead them into even more learning.

In the first week of school each student is provided with a blank student run chart to place in their individual data folder alongside their key concept list. The blank student run chart, Figure 14.1, can be downloaded free of charge from www.LBellJ.com.

After each quiz, students graph the number of correct items on their Student Run Chart. When students have at least one more correct answer than ever before they show their graph to both of the students operating the All-Time Best Distribution Center. "Teachers must stop over-emphasizing ability and start emphasizing progress (steep learning curves are the right of all students regardless of where they start)" (Hattie, 2009, p. 124).

One of the students provides a small dot or other sticker to place above the column with the highest score received thus far that year (Figure 14.2). You can count the six ATBs on the graph. The other student provides a shape for students to write their name on. (Figure 14.3)

Fig. 14.2

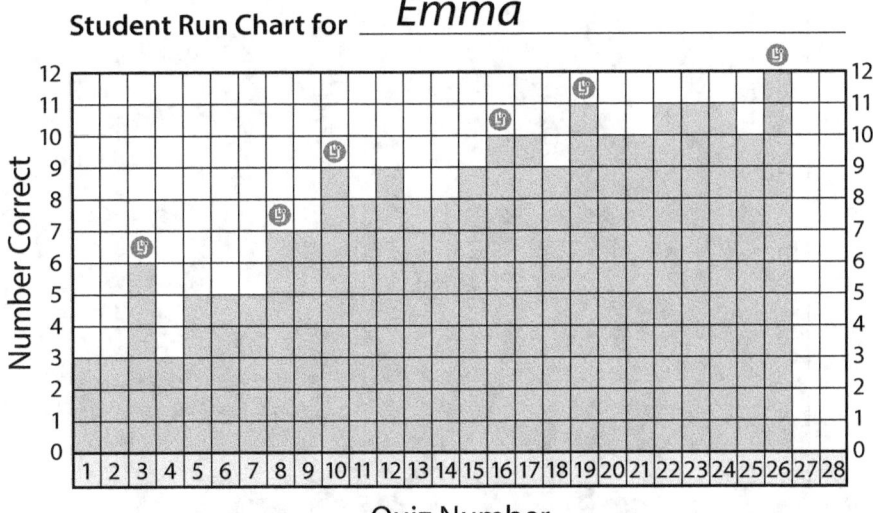

Fig. 14.3

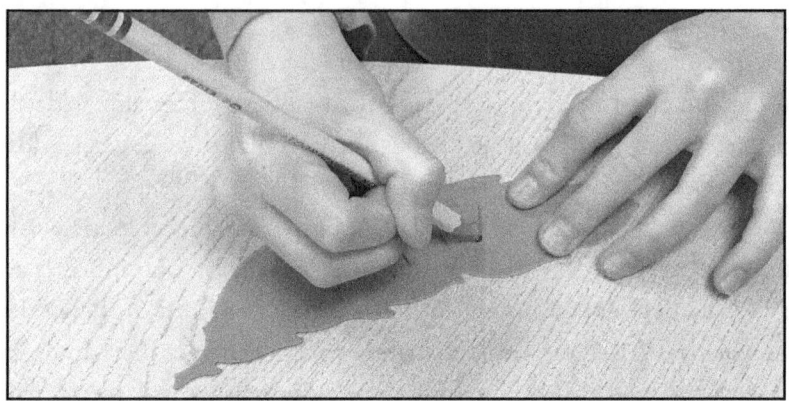

These shapes are placed on a wall or other visible space for all students to see and celebrate. Some schools even place their students' All-Time Best shapes in the hallways for all students and staff to see. The key part of the ATB process is to let the students drive the process, even deciding where to place the ATB shapes as in figure 14.5. Their creativity and leadership create ownership over their education.

Fig. 14.4

Fig. 14.5

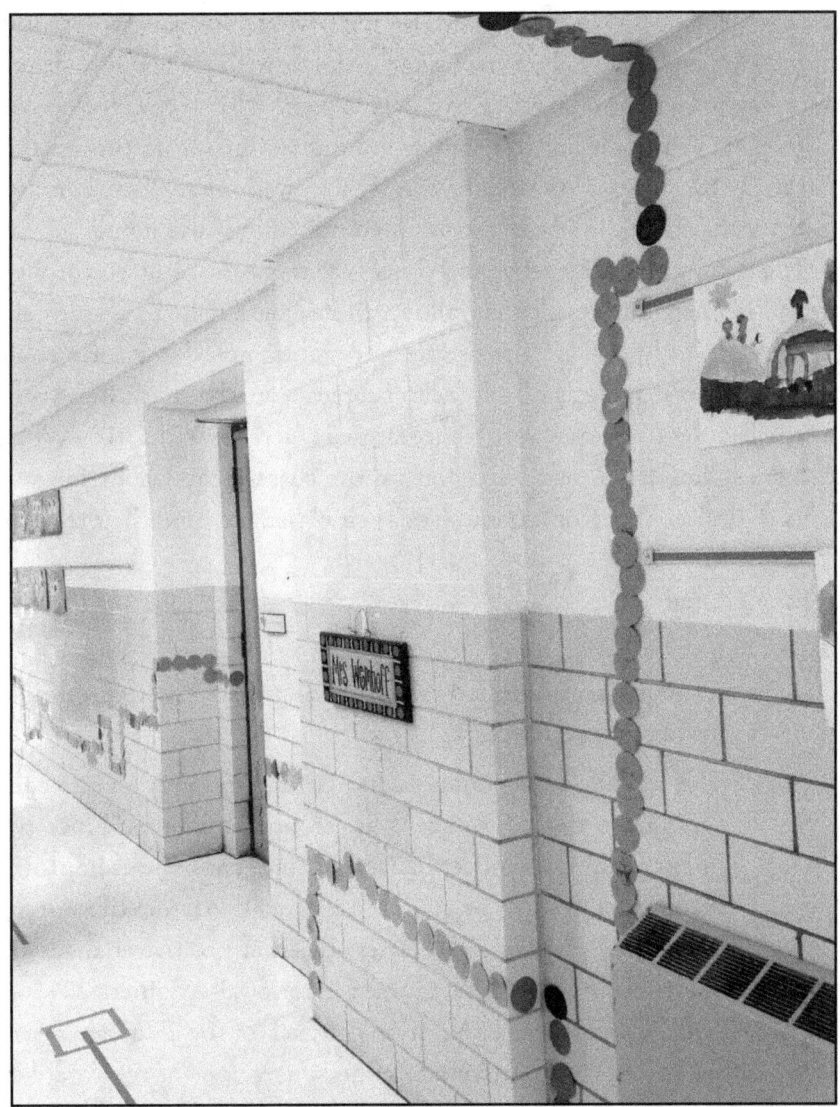

When you visit www.LBellJ.com and view the short minute video titled "Better Outcomes; Happier Kids," you will observe how Allan Culp,
Grade 7 history teacher in Anthem, Arizona, honors students who earn
an All-Time Best. They sign their name on the white board and then
they "high 10" their teacher. The ATB celebrations differ slightly from

elementary to secondary schools, but the heart inside all these students is the same; they like being honored for improving. Students are learning that "By applying yourself to the task of becoming a little better each and every day over a period of time, you will become a lot better" (Wooden, 1997, p. 11). "Habits are the compound interest of self-improvement" (Clear, 2018, p. 16). We are developing in children the attitude and evidence that they can have a record of continual improvement.

The details of the step-by-step process that was introduced through the ATB Distribution Center follow. These steps help us implement Deci's advice. He wrote, "The proper question is not, 'How can people motivate others?' but rather, 'How can people create the conditions within which others will motivate themselves?'" (Deci, 1995, p. 10). When teachers follow these steps, they create the correct conditions for students to desire more from themselves, their classmates and their teacher.

Step by step:

1. Students are informed of the surface-learning key concepts for the year (Chapter 13).

2. The teacher, seven times each quarter, randomly selects concepts from the key-concept list to quiz students. "Since the intent of the data collection is to advance continuous improvement, data need to be collected frequently to identify opportunities for change and to assess whether positive changes are in fact occurring" (Byrk, Gomez, Grunow, LeMahieu, 2015, p. 100). The number of questions on each of the 28 quizzes each school year is approximately the square root of the total key concepts for the whole year. Figure 14.1 is for 12 questions per quiz. One can assume that there are probably between 120 and 160 key concepts in a classroom utilizing this student run chart. Located at www.LBellJ.com are free blank graphs for 4, 5, 6, 7, 8, 10, 12, 16, 20, 24, 30, and 40 questions per quiz.

3. The quiz is administered just like any other quiz in the

classroom except students know it will not be graded. Some teachers who normally give graded quizzes prefer to use the term checks instead of quizzes.

4. The quiz is scored with the number of correct answers noted. All of the normal ways to indicate correct answers are utilized by various teachers.

5. Students graph their number of correct answers on the student run chart.

6. Students celebrate when they have an ATB by visiting the All-Time Best Distribution Center or some other process organized by the teacher. "Highlighting progress further builds a learner's sense of agency as he sees the relationship between his success and his actions" (Fisher, Frey, Hattie, 2016, p. 101).

7. Students record which key concepts they answered correctly on the key-concept list they were provided the first week of school (Chapter 13).

This process has at times been called review/preview because randomly selecting from the whole year's key concepts naturally brings up questions on content previously taught and content not-yet taught. When preview questions are on the quiz, teachers give a 15–30 second mini-explanation of the concept and estimate when the concept will be taught in depth. "Having some prior knowledge provides impetus for wanting to acquire even more knowledge" (Hattie and Yates, 2014, p. 7). We call this intrinsic motivation—the impetus for wanting to acquire even more knowledge.

Individual item analysis is accomplished by students recording correct answers. In grade 1, (figure 14.6), this can look like students highlighting correct spelling words, or recording a + or − for answers in Joni Ebel's middle school mathematics, (figure 14.7).

Sometimes teachers prepare the key concept list with spaces for + or − indicating a correct or incorrect answer for each item randomly selected for the quiz. Figure 14.8 shows an example created with Microsoft Word/insert table.

Fig. 14.6

Fig. 14.7

		5	Add & subtract decimals		6.1.3
		6	Use a plan to solve problems		6.1.3
		7	Multiply decimals		6.1.3
		8	Multiply & divide decimals with powers of 10		6.1.3a
		9	Divide decimals by whole numbers		6.1.3a
		10	Divide decimals by decimals		6.1.3a
		11	Use order of operations		6.3.3f
		12	Evaluate algebraic expressions		6.3.1c
		13	Translate words, phrases, and tables into algebraic expressions		6.3.1c
		14	Solve equations using addition, subtraction, multiplication & division		6.3.3a
		15	Identify and explain the properties of equality used in solving one step equations		6.3.3a
		16	Solve problems by using a specific method such as: writing an equation, make a table and look for a pattern, try, check, revise, draw a diagram, solve simpler problem, write an equation, make organized list, logical reasoning, work backward, make a graph		6.1.3.b 6.3.1.b
		17	Explain the multiplication property of equality (if a=b, then ac=bc)		6.3.3a
		18	Simplify exponential expressions		6.3.3.b
		19	Use scientific notation to represent very large numbers		6.1.1.d
		20	Use divisibility rules for 2, 3, 5, 6, 9, & 10		6.1.3.b
		21	Write the prime factorization of a number		6.1.1.e
		22	Find equivalent fractions		6.1.1.a
		23	Compare fractions		6.1.1.a
		24	Estimate sums and differences of fractions		6.1.4.a
		25	Add & subtract fractions with like denominators		6.1.2.a
		26	Add & subtract fractions with unlike denominators		6.1.2.a
		27	Add & subtract mixed numbers		6.1.2.a
		28	Solve equations with fractions using addition or subtraction		6.1.2.a
		29	Multiply & divide fractions		6.3.3.b

Fig. 14.8

Every suggestion in this chapter is written to reinforce a growth mindset in the mind of all students. We are not in a contest against others; we are in a contest against our former selves.

"Growth mindset . . . is not trying to prove we are better than others . . . instead they are constantly trying to improve" (Dweck, 2007, p. 110). When teachers test students on the essential key-concept list and ask them to document their ATBs along with the concepts they have been quizzed on, students are held accountable for their ability to learn and place content in their long-term memory. Because students are not in competition with others, they are more focused at the point of learning.

I have experienced the pain some students feel when they take their first LtoJ quiz the first week of school. These students realize they did not answer as many questions correctly as other students. Teachers reassure these students that the aim is to have one more correct answer than before. Selena Enriquez, in Ruidoso, NM, Grade 3, uses this process with the math fluency quizzes that are located at www.LBellJ.com. By the seventh week of school, students have taken seven math fluency quizzes. Every student in her class earned at least one ATB. Instead of the pain from public embarrassment continuing all year, as pointed out in Chapter 8, there is joy. Enriquez' experience, along with many others, supports the research finding reporting by John Hattie. He writes, "Andres Martin (2006) has shown the usefulness of this method, and how personal bests (PB) can improve enjoyment of learning, participation in class, and persistence on the task . . . PB's relate to the attainment of a personalized standard and this is what distinguishes them from many other goals. They are competitive (relative to previous bests) and self-improving (success leads to enhanced performance)" (Hattie, 2012, p. 55).

Honoring each student's All-Time Best each time they improve their score shows students how important it is to focus on what each student is capable of individually. Honoring each time the student or the class collectively reaches their All-Time Best reinforces that each student is a vital part of the classroom team. While this process may seem time consuming at first, once students become confident in the process and feel the joy of success early in the year, teachers see how vital it is to implement an All-Time Best Distribution Center. By acknowledging small improvements, teachers will see massive gains in both confidence and knowledge retention.

Finally, please approach all of the student improvement with a sense of gratitude towards students. We adults teach, but the students have control over whether or not they learn. When they do learn, we are grateful. "Ingratitude is one of the most disliked traits in people. It acts as a repellent. No one wants to be around ingrates. Gratitude, on the other hand, is right up there in the top ten percent of qualities people appreciate" (Newmark and Norville, 2016, introduction).

CHAPTER 15

We Did it—Because of Me!

*Learning is often "in the head" and an aim of the teacher
is to help make this learning visible.*

John Hattie

A graph is a tool for data visualization, a picture that tells a story.

Ben Orlin

Daktronics, a Brookings, South Dakota firm, has had major commercial success manufacturing the huge digital scoreboards so popular at many athletic events. Scoreboards are not a new idea but the jumbo screens clearly add to people's overall enjoyment of the game. The foundation for both modern and former scoreboards, is the same—addition. The scores contributed by each player are added up for a team score. Addition is all that's needed.

However, it is common for many high-school athletic coaches to also serve as teachers in the classroom. The head football coach is also the science teacher. Each Friday night when he walks across the gridiron he expects to see a scoreboard keeping track of the game's progress.

Yet, he teaches science year after year with no classroom scoreboard in sight—no addition of the contributions of each student. There is no team score for the classroom. Students do not get to watch their contributions add to the success of the classroom. We need to change this, as team scores are a major contributor to increasing intrinsic motivation. Our students and teachers must see their progress daily to encourage them to continue showing up every day—trying harder than they did the day before.

> **... team scores are a major contributor to increasing intrinsic motivation.**

The essence of Part III is collecting feedback from students so as to inform teacher leadership of learning. The elements that comprise leadership of learning are feedback from students to teachers, celebrations for improvement and student-generated hypotheses to improve learning. The process and the three classroom graphs are all feedback to the teacher answering the questions, "Are my students placing the essential key concepts into their long-term memory?" and "Are students on track to meet end-of-the-year standards?" Leaders of classroom learning need this information constantly.

The first step for this feedback, the classroom team data, is to collect the information from each member of the class. Since there is no outside scorekeeper recording the results, as in athletic events, the students record the data themselves. I learned the simplest way to collect this data from Allen Culp, who teaches in Anthem, Arizona. He placed tape on a small portion of his whiteboard for students to merely make a dot indicating their number of correct answers on the quiz. Figure 15.1 shows his data

Fig. 15.1

10		
9		
8	• •	16
7	• •	14
6	• • •	18
5	• • • •	20
4	• •	8
3	• • • •	12
2	• •	4
1	•	1
0	•	0

collector and 15.2 is the same from Angie Romero's Grade 2 classroom in Ruidoso, New Mexico. Her adaptation is laminated chart paper. (The numerals to the right on figure 15.1 are the result of multiplication as a step toward adding up the total correct answers for the class.)

Fig. 15.2

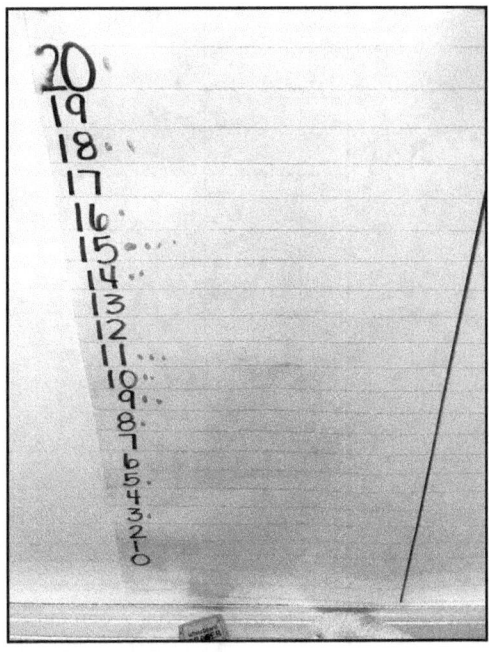

Placing the dot on the collector concludes the third data responsibility completed by every student. In chapter 14 I explained (1) the individual student run chart and (2) the individual item analysis. Next, pairs of students are assigned the responsibility of completing three graphs making classroom learning visible—the scatter diagram, the histogram, and the class run chart.

Each of these three blank graphs can be downloaded for free from www.LBellJ.com.

Students create all of the graphs; they love the responsibility. It takes about five minutes to explain to six students how to create the graphs—two students for the scatter diagram, two students for the histogram, and two students for the class run chart. This explanation occurs once each school year. When it is time for students to take a turn creating these graphs, one of each pair of students is tasked to teach the new students. The teacher never needs to explain how to create these graphs again in the year. Students take their responsibilities very seriously for both creating graphs and teaching others about them.

The three free blank graphs for classroom data are shown in figures 15.3, 15.4, and 15.5.

Fig. 15.3

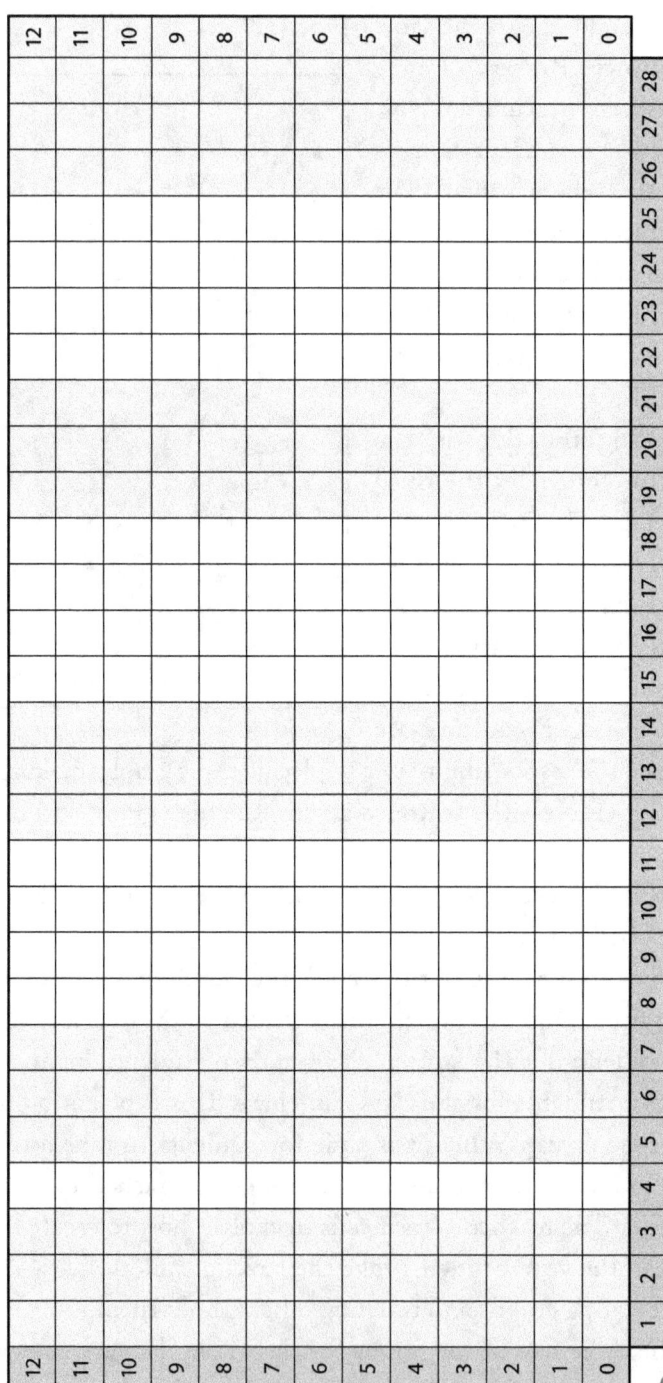

Scatter Diagram

Fig. 15.4

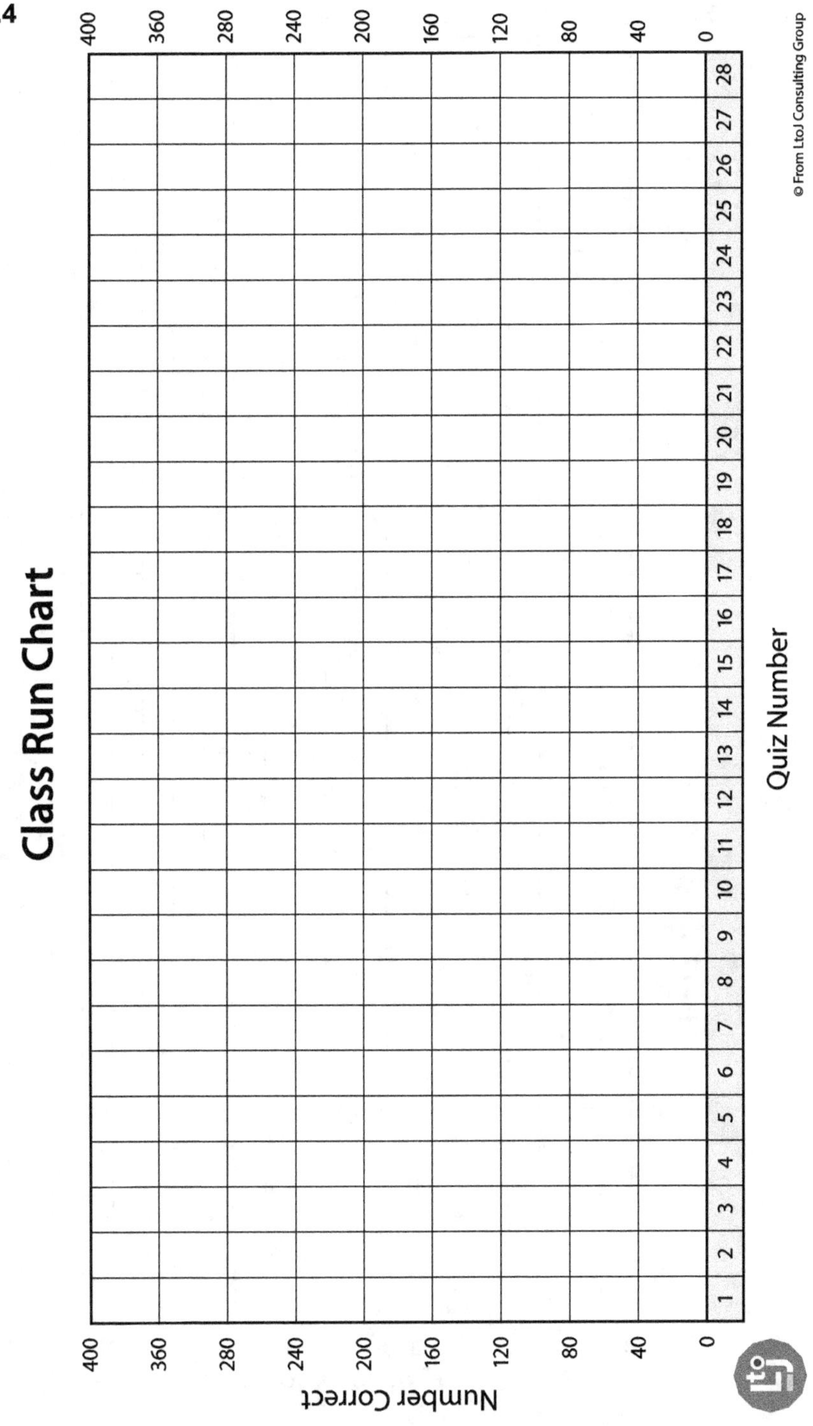
Class Run Chart
Number Correct
400
360
280
240
200
160
120
80
40
0
1 2 3 4 5 6 7 8 9 10 11 12 13 14 15 16 17 18 19 20 21 22 23 24 25 26 27 28
Quiz Number
© From LtoJ Consulting Group

Fig. 15.5

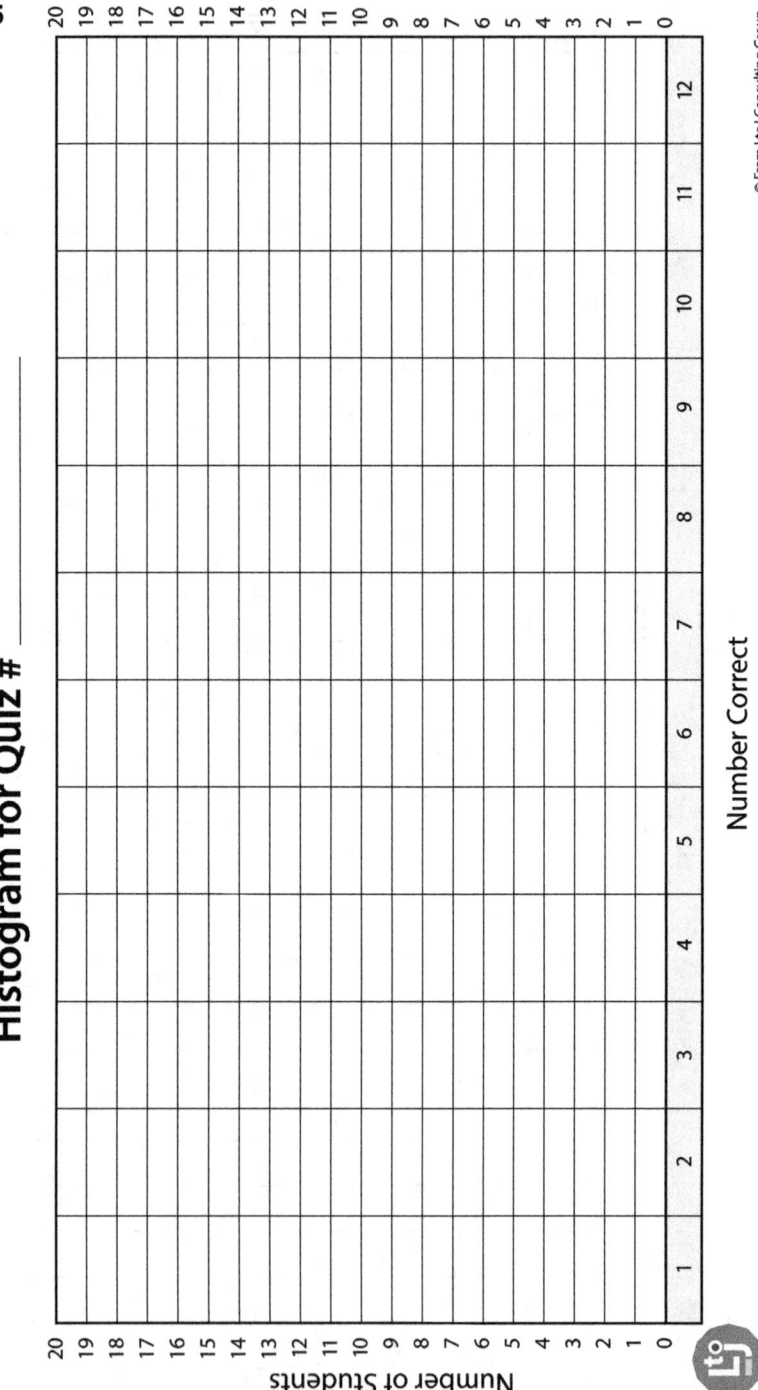

Histogram for Quiz # _____

Number of Students

Number Correct

The samples in this chapter are for 12-question quizzes. A class using the 12-item graphs probably has between 120 and 160 key concepts on their list. On www.LbellJ.com select between multiple sets of graphs based upon number of questions per quiz.

The class run chart is like the scoreboard at athletic events— simple addition.

The scatter diagram simply records the dots on the collector shown in Figures 15.1 and 15.2. The shaded columns are the data that will be used for calculating effect size using the LtoJ Effect-Size-Calculator explained in Chapter 18. This data becomes one of the most effective forms of student assessment: effect size. Without the scatter diagram, this powerful, significant feedback is significantly more difficult for teachers and students to collect.

The class run chart is like the scoreboard at athletic events—simple addition. It is the total correct answers for each of the 28 quizzes completed each academic year. Students perform all of the addition. When the numerals are larger, such as with the math fluency quizzes, the recommendation is that the two students completing the class run chart look at the dots on the collector and enter the numerals into Excel. At a very young age they can learn to use the SUM command. Giving students these techniques empowers them and establishes skills that will serve them for the rest of their life.

The histogram is the graph from which the name LtoJ is derived. In the beginning of the year, the ideal histogram is in the shape of an *L*, in the middle of the year we have the famous bell curve and at the end of the year the desire is a *J* curve. At the end of Jack Canfield's interview of me, located at www.LBellJ.com, are pictures of the L, bell, and J curves. To make the histogram, students look at the collector and color in columns on the graph. The histogram is the only one of the three classroom graphs that requires a new blank graph each quiz. Without the histogram, students do not see their classroom learning progress from the L to the bell and onto the J.

Once the three graphs are completed, the dots on the collector are erased and it is ready for the next quiz.

Fig. 15.6

Figure 15.6 shows the simple display of the three graphs from Angie Romero's Grade 2 classroom in Ruidoso, New Mexico. Three sheet protectors have been adhered to a closet door to hold the graphs. As soon as all the dots are on the collector, the assigned students swing into action and have their jobs completed very quickly. "Sharing a common understanding of progression is the most critical success factor in any school" (Hattie, 2012, p. 67).

In his book, *Atomic Habits*, James Clear tells a story from the Netherlands regarding the use of electricity. The problem was that homes that were exactly the same had huge discrepancies in their use of power. The researchers found that the only difference between the houses was the location of the electrical meter. Homes with the meter inside the house, where it was observed continually, used far less power than homes where the meter was located outside the house. Students do pay attention to the graphs, especially so when the teacher comments, "Did you notice that our histogram is starting to show a *J*?

Below are three pictures from Angela Willnerd's Fremont, Nebraska classroom—one of each of the three graphs. I determined a number of years ago to not computerize these graphs; the students are very engaged with this process and the creativity is quite amazing. When you go to www.visiblelearningplus.com and look at the research by clicking on the command for the two-page PDF you will see either "self-reported grades" or "assessment-capable students." These two labels are synonyms for the same research: students understand in detail the assessment results.

Fig. 15.7

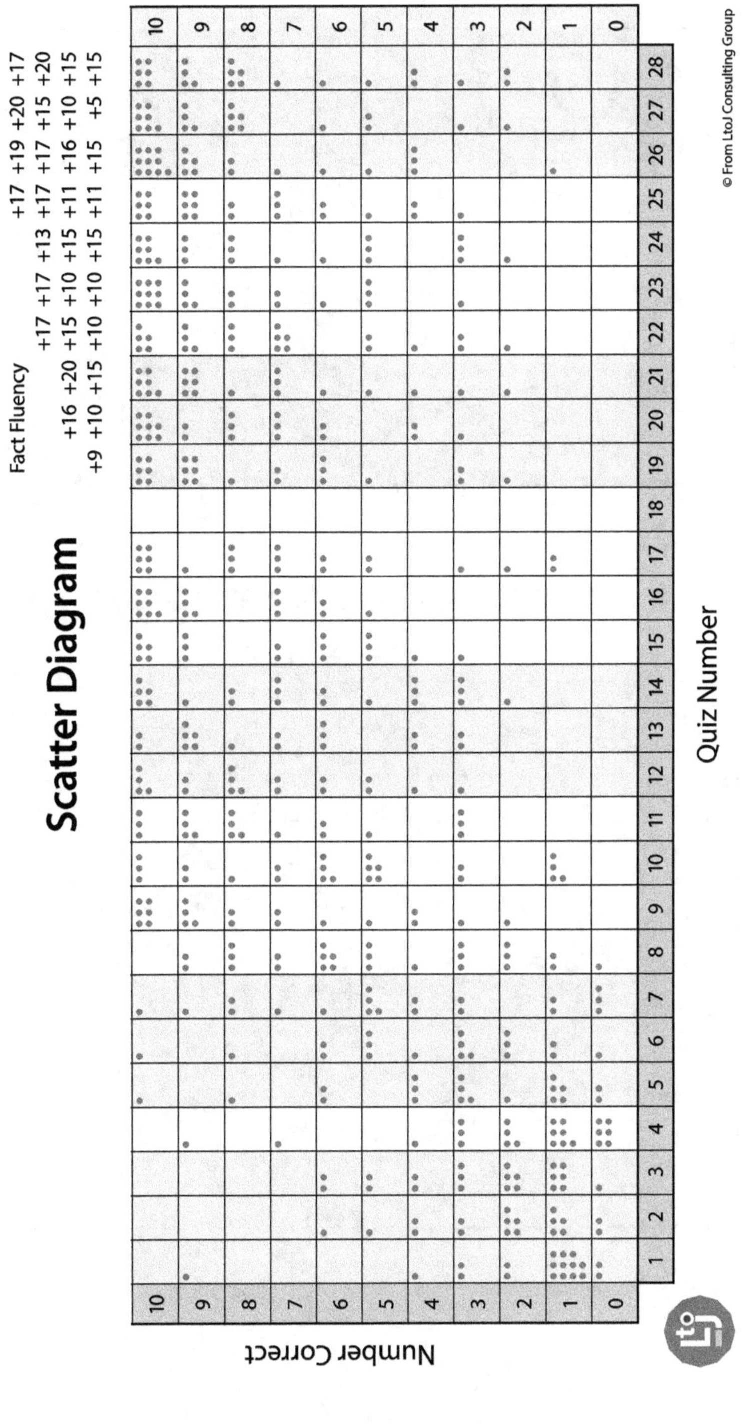

Scatter Diagram

Fact Fluency

+17 +19 +20 +17
+17 +17 +17 +15 +20
+17 +17 +13 +17 +15 +10 +15
+17 +17 +10 +15 +11 +16 +10 +15
+16 +20 +15 +10 +10 +15 +11 +15 +5 +15
+9 +10 +15 +10

Number Correct

Quiz Number

Fig. 15.8

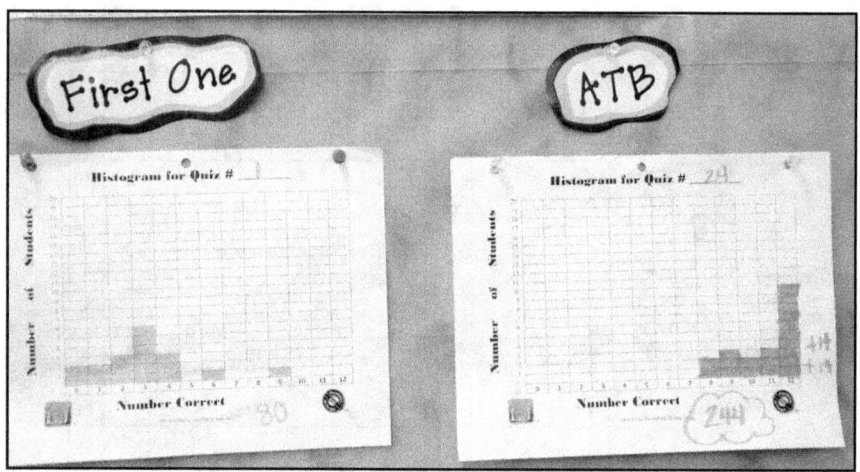

Fig. 15.9

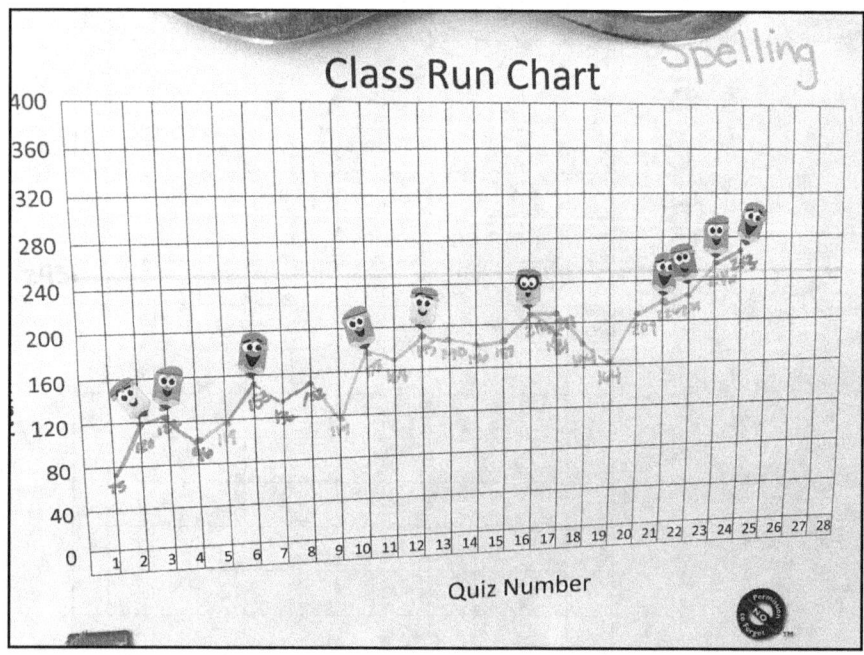

Learning is tripled when the classroom is full of assessment-capable students who know what they are to learn for the year, what they know thus far, and how the class as a whole is progressing. On the scatter diagram from Mrs. Willnerd's classroom are notations of extra numerals in the upper right. These are the scores for students who were accelerated to the next grade level in math fluency. This is explained further in Chapter 25.

One of my favorite inadvertent benefits that occurs when using this data collection process involves the class run chart. Occasionally a class beats their All-Time Best by only one or two correct answers. A student who generally struggles to be successful blurts out for all to hear, "It was because of me that we had a class ATB! My two correct answers pushed us over the top. We all get to celebrate because of me!" Think about this compared to awards assemblies where the same few are honored year after year. Here, everybody contributes to the learning, everybody celebrates, and everybody has visual evidence of (1) their personal learning and (2) their contribution to the success of the whole class.

This joy should not be surprising. We know the story from sports. Imagine that a mediocre athlete is put into the basketball game and makes a one-point free throw. The team then wins by one point. The mediocre athlete tells everyone it was his/her one point that won the game. The same experience occurs over and over in classrooms. Jeff Burgard's Grade 8 science class accomplished an ATB by one point because a new student arrived in his classroom and answered one question correctly on her first day in the new school. "Welcome to our class; we are glad you are here. Without you we would have not obtained an ATB." What could have been a stressful and lonely first day turned into a day of celebration for a new student, and a class full of students to have a new member on their learning team. "All the qualities that have been traditionally and erroneously applied to competition actually apply better to cooperation. Cooperation builds character, is basic to human nature, and makes learning more enjoyable and productive" (Deming, 1994, p. 152).

Readers may have noticed that the scatter diagram and run charts (student and class) are all designed for 28 quizzes a school year. The reason for 28 is that teachers state seven times a quarter is doable, whereas trying to do it every week invites failure. "Habits are based upon frequency, not upon time" (Clear, 2018, p. 145).

When a class reaches an All-Time Best, it only makes sense to have a celebration. Just as when a sports team wins a game and the crowd cheers them off the field, students need to be acknowledged for their hard work and accomplishments. Pink expressed, "Only contingent rewards—if you do this, then you'll get that—had the negative effect. Why? 'If then' rewards require people to forfeit some of their autonomy" (Pink, 2009, p. 38). Everybody, even very young children, knows the difference between an "if-then" statement and the celebrations given freely for simply doing better than ever before. These are not the usual bribes that students encounter using expired teaching methods. Celebrations are quick, fun, and involve the entire class. Teachers communicate this message saying, "We will have All-Time Bests. Guaranteed. And when we do, we will all celebrate. All of us. It will be for fun; I will not be giving you pizza, candy, or anything else. Fun will be the celebration."

The bonus part of the LtoJ process is watching how creative teachers become when thinking of ways to celebrate with their students. They are following Batterson's advice: "Don't accumulate possessions; accumulate experiences" (Batterson, 2006, p. 43). The possessions of pizza, doughnuts, trinkets, and awards are quickly forgotten; the celebrations are not.

1. Take everybody's picture using the photo booth app on many phones, project the pictures, and laugh. A variation is the photo booth pictures are all of the high school teachers.

2. Sing a song with rounds such as Tooty Ta. After each ATB, the class sings the song, adding one new motion. Start with only one motion for the first ATB and add a new motion for each new ATB. By the end of the year it can be wild.

3. Provide two minutes for students to flip their water bottles.

4. Play a number of games with the Hasbro game "Bop it."

5. The teacher twirls a baton, does cartwheels, or something else that causes students to laugh.

6. Watch a short, very humorous gag video from YouTube.

Celebrations by the whole team are not unusual for athletics, music, or theatre. Now, simply because of addition in the classroom all students are celebrated in all classrooms. "The future will be all about sharable moments" (Kramer, 2016, p. 188).

The classrooms may not have a jumbotron to project the All-Time Bests each time, but there are a variety of fun and easy ways to collect data and celebrate student, classroom, and even whole-school ATBs. Principal Laura Sulzbach organized a time for her teachers to switch classrooms for five minutes and share a favorite story to celebrate her school's All-Time Best.

Such a basic celebration turned out to be one that was a favorite for teachers, students, and me. When we celebrate our students' contributions to their own learning and to the school as a whole, we see a greater buy-in. They are enthusiastic participants in their education. By empowering them to collect and analyze their own data, teachers create leaders not only in the classroom, but in their schools. These young leaders will continue to move mountains because they start to hear in their school, "You make a difference. We cannot get better without you."

CHAPTER 16

No Game No More

Getting an "A" measures that the student "knows how to play the game of school." It does NOT always demonstrate real mastery of material.

Jessica Lahey

I was trying to avoid this conversation, but failed. Here I was in the doctor's office in my underwear for my annual dermatology exam. The doctor asked, "What do you do for a living?"

I replied, "I get on airplanes and go various places, pick up a microphone and make presentations."

"Who is your audience?" she asked.

"Teachers and administrators," I replied while thinking, *I want this over so I can get dressed.*

"What do you tell them?" she continued.

"I tell them how to set up schools so students have to actually learn. They can no longer cram, get their grade, and then forget," was my simple answer.

"Very interesting," the doctor replied. "That's all I did in school, even in medical school."

I was wondering how this was going to end up. *Here I am in a medical office with a doctor telling me she crammed and forgot all the way through medical school.* So I asked, "You have to learn everything sometime, don't you?"

"That's what residency is for," was her straightforward answer.

Soon I was able to get dressed, but then I had a stomachache. All the way from Grade 1 through medical school education is merely a game.

I was trusting my health and well-being to someone who may or may not remember the right answers because she crammed her way through school. But then I thought, *This must be an anomaly*, and on an airplane flight shortly thereafter my seatmate happened to be an MD. I told him of my conversation with my dermatologist and asked him for his analysis. He said, "You heard correctly. That is the way it goes." The pit in my stomach returned and it was not from airplane turbulence.

And then there is the conversation with a high-ranking leader in K–12 education. This educator was frustrated by the stories his children were bringing home from their school. So, I asked, "What are you telling your kids?"

"Play the game. Do everything the teachers ask. This is how you get the scholarships for college," was the reply. Even people who have spent years in the education profession do not know how to help their students or their very own children navigate the system other than to play the game.

On another flight I sat next to a software company trainer. Her corporation sells software to other businesses and she is then brought in to train the new customers on the use of the software. Intrigued by her job description, I stated, "Wow, that seems like a great job."

She replied, "I hate my job," which caused me to ask a surprised, "Why?"

"The salespeople lie. They promise software features we do not have. The salespeople collect their commission and I am the one to inform the purchaser that the expected software feature is not available." The software salespeople are gaming the system.

From this conversation it became all the more evident that the problem with the education system is affecting more than just education, it is affecting customers, patients, parents, and more. This is a widespread, overlapping problem, and gaming the system is becoming far too normal.

There are approximately 50 million students in kindergarten through twelfth grade in the United States. If it costs an average of $11,000 per student per year, that is a whopping 540 billion dollars per year. The investment is well worth it, but not if education is only a game. I am well aware that there are teachers who structure their classrooms so students actually learn and there is no thought of education being a game in their classes. The students learn. However, the system reinforces the message to students that they only need to learn for the year and then they are free to forget again.

The students think, "Who needs algebra 1? I am in geometry now," or "I am sure glad I do not need to remember US History while I am in World History." The lack of consistency and a failure to build upon prior knowledge makes learning a game that can only be temporarily won.

We can change our current system from a forgetting system to a remembering system! "If you want better results, then forget about setting goals. Focus on your system instead" (Clear, 2018, p. 24). Let's stop blaming summer. "The so-called 'summer effect,' whereby students reduce achievement over summer is probably as much the result of 'holding' back by new teachers as they reassess to make their own judgements as it is of the students having been on holiday (Hattie, 2012, p. 65).

Schools were not always set up for forgetting. I have talked to a number of people who either taught in a one-room country school or attended such a school. They all tell the same story. Forgetting was very unlikely because you always heard last year's content taught to a younger student and you always heard next year's content taught to an older student. The preview helped students remember because they were given a clear idea of what was coming up next year. Because this remembering was unintentional, nobody figured out how to structure a system that supports remembering as pupil population increased and schools instituted separate classrooms for each grade level and each subject in middle and high school.

Further, when people looked at the content to be learned, they were not statisticians, so they inadvertently structured schools for forgetting. It all started with spelling in Grade 1.

Students are given a list of 12 words a week to learn. They take a test on Friday over the 12 words and every Monday are given a new list. It is assumed that the students will remember those 12 words, but they are never retested on them. The teachers never tell their students they can forget last week's words, but students soon learn the game. They learn that all they have to do is cram for four days, regurgitate those words on Friday, forget those words over the weekend in order to make room for new words on Monday. This practice, as noted earlier, continues on through medical school.

Using the LtoJ process eradicates the option to forget previously learned knowledge. Students in Grade 6 science class, for example, are given a list of 130 key concepts to learn. They know that is too many items to cram. They are told they will have all year to learn the concepts and that there will be no need to cram. Instead they are told they will have a weekly quiz on 12 of the 130 concepts, randomly selected most weeks. The quiz will be non-graded and can include any material listed on the key concepts provided for the whole year. It does not matter if the content has been taught or not.

It took a statistician, W. Edwards Deming, to figure out how to assess in a way that is not a game. I would never on my own think of random assessment of long-term memory. I knew non-random assessment of short-term memory did not work, but did not know the alternative until Deming made the suggestion. "We need evidence to help us discern whether any specific changes attempted are actually improvements" (Byrk, 2015, p. 475). Random assessment gives us the needed evidence in minimal time.

Further, these students are informed that when they are in Grade 7, they will be asked mostly Grade 7 questions, but also a few Grade 5 and 6 questions each week. They do not have permission to forget the prior content when in Grade 7. So, when these students are in Grade 8 and on into high school, there will always be questions from prior grade levels. Always. No game, no more. Figure 16.1 is from a Grade 3 classroom where spelling is no longer a game. The three buckets are for Grade 3 words, Grade 2 words, and Grade 1 words. Spelling is taught in a logical manner, but the assessment is random, with sixteen words drawn randomly from the third bucket, three from the second bucket and one from the first bucket for the weekly spelling test. This creates long-term assessment for all spelling quizzes. Accurate knowledge

Fig. 16.1

comes from assessment of long-term memory. No more game. No more being fooled by assessments of short-term memory. Accurate knowledge comes from assessment of long-term memory. "Assessment of students is a powerful way to learn about your impact" (Hattie and Yates, 2014, p. 69). Another way of explaining this is "Improvement research calls for data, not for purposes of ranking individuals, or organizations, but for learning how well specific processes actually work" (Byrk, Gomez, Grunow, LeMahieu, 2015, p. 187). Students have to continually prove that they learned the material, and cannot play the cram and forget game anymore.

When students remember the content from current and former courses there is no need to cram prior to exams. Students learn to trust the teachers when they say that every surface-learning question on the graded exams will be based on the key-concept list provided the first week of the school year. Further, there is a way to follow the same principles for graded finals as is utilized with the non-graded LtoJ quizzes. Because the game is played to garner good grades without having to learn, it is essential to spend some time on graded exams.

Students in LtoJ classrooms are expected to take final exams, but how these exams are created and what they ask differs from a traditional exam. Many secondary teachers in both middle and high school are pleased with giving their end-of-the-year, graded final, four times a year. It is given at first quarter, semester, third quarter, and end of the year. The change is that students are only expected to answer 25% correctly at first quarter, 50% at semester, 75% at third quarter and 100% at the end of the year. If a teacher had a 100-item final, then at nine weeks a perfect score would be 25 questions correct. In the computerized grading program, the teacher would not enter 100 questions, but rather 25 as the total number of questions. Remember, this 100-item final has 60 questions from the current year and 40 questions from prior grade levels. So, all students need to do to have an A on the exam at first quarter is remember prior years. By semester, students would need to remember prior years and some of the new year.

In high school, students cannot earn As by studying one chapter of a book the night before the chapter test. There is NO GAME, NO MORE. All graded exams should be of long-term memory. Students will change their mindset about school when they realize that in chemistry class they will have graded questions from biology, physical science, earth science, and general science all the way back to Grades 5 or 6. They know they cannot cram that much, but will feel very smart when they know they can learn that much.

Teachers say, "But I want to know if they learned what I taught this week." Right now, teachers are fooled. It is legitimate to want to know if students learned what you taught this week, but a chapter test does not tell you. Teachers are fooled by the game—the cramming process. It is only when the content of the current week is assessed multiple weeks later that teachers will know if the content has truly been mastered.

Just in case you think this chapter pertains mainly to elementary school, listen to Michael Clay Thompson. He writes about teaching high-school English stating, "I do not teach anything—especially a book—as a self-contained unit. I am convinced that as soon as students perceive a unit to have concluded, they discard its intellectual contents . . . If you tell them the first novel will not be included on the second novel's test, you are telling them it's over. When it's over for the teacher, it's over for the kids (Thompson, 1995, p. 61).

CHAPTER 17

Everybody Loves Feeling Smart

In order to really nail that memory down, we must tag it for retrieval later on. This final part of the process, retrieval, is vital to learning because it solidifies knowledge through the process of pulling the information out of the brain in order to apply it to novel situations and contexts.
Jessica Lahey

After working alongside the middle- and high-school science teachers for a couple of days I counted the number of unduplicated key concepts for all required science courses. The number was slightly over 300. The teachers removed trivia from their lists; only the essential science key concepts for surface-learning remained. Then I asked the science teachers how they would feel at graduation if they knew that all of the students crossing the stage, receiving their diplomas, had these 300+ key concepts solidified in their long-term memory. I asked, "Isn't this a low expectation? Only a little over 300 key concepts for five or more years of science?" The answer was exactly what I expected. The teachers would be thrilled knowing students had so much science embedded into their long-term memory, especially because now they suspect that their students remember very little.

Nobody finishes a course remembering nothing and still feels smart. Nobody. The foundation for feeling smart is remembering. There is certainly more to being smart than remembering, but remembering is the essential foundation for intelligence. Our science teachers have this sinking feeling that very few of their graduates feel smart in science. Which means that almost everything they have spent the entire five years teaching is wasted.

Let's look at John Hattie's learning triangle again (Figure 17.1). When people feel smart, they (1) remember the surface-learning, (2) easily retrieve surface-learning

Nobody finishes a course remembering nothing and still feels smart.

to solve deep-learning problems and (3) can transfer both surface and deep learning to other school subjects and out-of-school experiences. One of the major reasons I recommend almost no time on review at the beginning of the school year is so teachers will have time to teach new content well. The current year's surface-learning is far too often taught in a rush. In fact, the word teach is not used when teachers are in a rush; the word is "cover." "When teachers race through curriculum materials at a faster than normal pace, then deep learning is affected dramatically" (Hattie and Yates, 2014, p. 47). Students are left wading in the deep end of content they do not understand.

I completely comprehend why many educators tend to discount the value of surface- learning. Their experiences as students were memorizing mostly trivia from a textbook chapter. Never did they have a teacher who clearly wrote out the essential key concepts and then held them accountable for only the essential and never the trivial. I can only think

Fig. 17.1

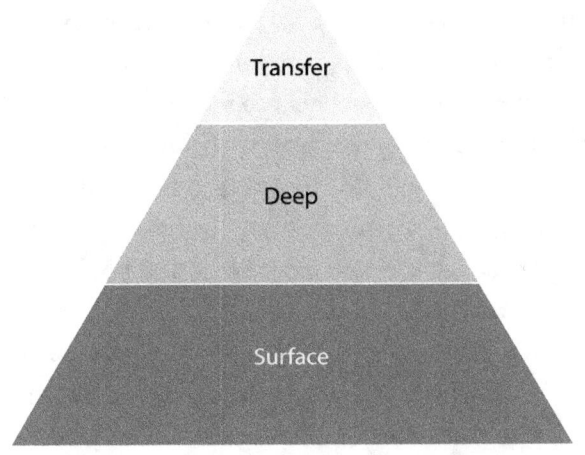

of one reason for assessing students on trivia. When teachers grade on a curve, they need trivia in order to rank students for grades. When teachers desire 10% As, 15% Bs, 50% Cs, 15% Ds and 10% Fs, trivia is the perfect tool. When students are in courses where the grading curve is used, they understand that a C is the highest grade possible without cramming trivia.

The better choice for teachers is grading based upon learning essentials. Because students are informed of the surface-learning for the year during the first week, they know that the first step towards feeling smart in the class is to gradually place the year-long surface-learning into long-term memory. The students know that all graded assessments of surface-learning will be composed of questions derived from this list with no trick questions. They also know what percentage of the final grade is based upon surface-learning and what percentage on deep and transfer-learning.

There is more to feeling smart than surface-learning. Deep and transfer learning follow.

In Chapter 25 two students were given a deep-learning assignment to determine the percentage of the classroom walls covered by paper because the fire marshal was coming. Successful students with this deep-learning assignment rely upon earlier surface-learning with both percentages and area measurement. They are then able to apply their past knowledge to the current problem.

Hattie and Yates caution us by writing, "Teaching someone a new skill and then expecting that person to immediately apply it within a new and complex situation is asking too much" (Hattie and Yates, 2014, p. 152). Educators should never stop with surface-learning but should push students onto deeper learning that requires understanding and remembering of surface-learning. It may be wise for teachers to assign deep-learning tasks for the first portion of a school year based upon surface-learning from prior years.

When teachers rely mostly upon textbooks, it may seem like the text is providing both surface and deep-learning. After all, the chapter has directions for area calculations, practice, and then word problems. The word problems are for deep-learning. Correct? My experience with most of these word problems is that they are really surface-learning problems with words instead of numerals. In order for deep-learning to occur students need to apply surface-learning to real-life problems, not with fake data.

After the key concepts for surface-learning are written and given to students, teachers then brainstorm with others on deep-learning questions for each surface-learning key concept.

Examples for deep-learning questions to follow surface-learning instruction on computation of area follow:

1. What percentage of the campus is covered by grass?
2. What percentage of a basketball court is outside the three-point line?
3. What percentage of the classroom is covered by carpet? By tile?
4. How many more square feet in the kindergarten room than in the other classrooms?
5. How many square feet in our classroom is open space, not covered by desks or tables?

All of these examples involve the environment and current life. This is a requirement for the most successful deep-learning. "Learning proceeds quietly and efficiently when what is new builds upon what is already secured" (Hattie and Yates, 2014, p. 126)

Another way to cause students to dig deeper is to provide assignments with constraints. "To spur real creativity, a puzzle needs constraints" (Orlin, 2018, p. 12). This can be as simple as: The paragraph you write to answer the assigned question must have five sentences only. One sentence is to have three words, one sentence is to have four words, one to have five words, one to have six words, and one to have seven words. Orlin writes further, "Creativity is what happens when a mind encounters an obstacle. It's the human process of finding a way through, over, around, or beneath. No obstacle, no creativity" (Orlin, p. 13).

Evidence of transfer-learning is one of the major ways adults know intrinsic motivation is being maintained. When students recognize they can transfer learning from one class to another class or from school to outside-school experiences, they feel smart! On one of my visits to Allan Culp's seventh grade social studies class in Anthem, Arizona, I drew Hattie's triangle for surface, deep, and transfer-learning on the whiteboard. I quickly defined the three levels, explaining that their LtoJ quizzes were surface-learning. We discussed some deep-learning occurring within their classroom, but the majority of time was occupied with transfer-learning. I was surprised. All of the Grade 7 teachers provided the students key-concept lists for the year and were utilizing the LtoJ process to receive feedback on student learning. The students were eager to share with me how often they transferred learning between each of the four core classes of social studies, English, science, and mathematics. They felt so smart telling me about all this transfer-learning.

I have divided Hattie's learning triangle into halves in order to help educators plan more efficiently (Figure 17.2). The two segments of surface-learning are essential key concepts and automaticity. Most of what is essential needs to be available in the brain for deep-learning problems

Fig. 17.2

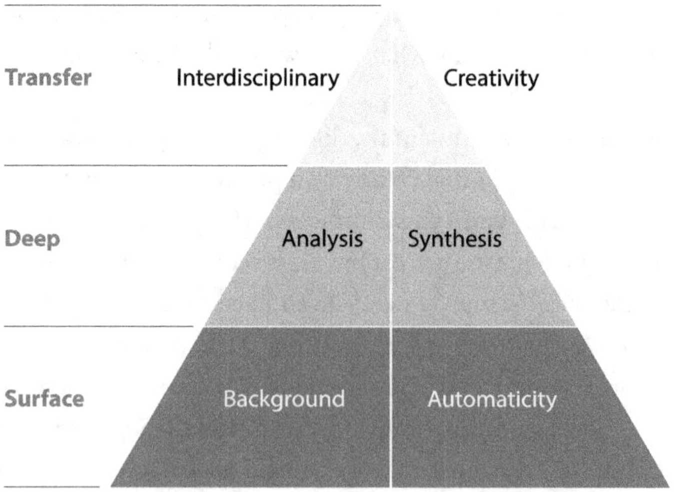

but does not need to be recalled instantly. Automaticity is for the items that do need to be recalled instantly. "Speed of access in memory functions strongly predicts two other attributes: confidence and positive feelings" (Hattie and Yates, p. 59). "Bloom referred to automaticity as the 'hands and feet of genius'" (Hattie and Yates, p. 97). Below is a limited, side-by-side listing of essential key concepts and automaticity.

Subject	Sample Essential	Sample Automatic
Social Studies	What happens in state capitals	Locate USA states –blank map
Language arts	Various literary definitions	Conventions for writing
Mathematics	Length, weight, volume, formulas	Number facts

Hattie and Yates lamented, "Strangely enough, we really do not have a great deal of knowledge on how to teach for automaticity" (2014, p. 59). The title of Chapter 8, strangely enough, had to do with math fluency quizzes. It may be that the reason we do not have a great deal of knowledge on how to teach for automaticity is we are looking for teaching research, when the problem is most likely psychology. Students are ranked and embarrassed by math fluency progress instead of receiving credit for improvement and subsequent celebrations. We hold students back from moving on until they "master" what is first on the list. My nephew, Eric McConnaughey, remembers that in kindergarten he never was asked to learn his address because he couldn't spell for all of kindergarten his last name.

On my expansion of Hattie's triangle, deep is divided into analysis and synthesis. All *How to Create a Perfect School* readers and I share this in common: we all use analysis and synthesis in our lives. We desire the same for our students and our family members. In the writing of this book both are used. An example of each follows.

"Analysis is breaking an idea down into its components. Are there different types of characters? Does the protagonist go through several states of personal development?" (Thompson, 1995, p. 53). The definition of analysis by Thompson is generic and true for all aspects of education. The two questions are ones he would ask his students in English.

For years I studied how to improve student success in elementary mathematics. My analysis caused me to observe that struggling math students did not see the patterns. The students who were successful in math immediately saw the patterns, and the others were trying to remember a formula. For example, I was talking to two brothers, one in Grade 3 who loved math and one in Grade 5 who had the opposite opinion. I asked the Grade 5 brother what six times eight was. He looked up in the air, feigning thinking, and gave me a wrong answer. The younger brother said that four sixes equaled 24 and therefore eight sixes had to be double that. So the answer is 48. The analysis continued. Why don't all students see the patterns? I cannot say why some students see the patterns and others do not. I did see, however, that patterns normally are not a part of the instructional materials provided to schools.

How to Create a Perfect School is more about synthesis than analysis, even though there is a lot of analysis present. "Synthesis is combining separate ideas into one new idea, identifying similarities. Making connections" (Thompson, p. 50). The synthesis of *How to Create a Perfect School* is orchestrating the profound writing of John Hattie, Carol Dweck, and W. Edwards Deming, plus others, into one cohesive book. I started on this journey through reading and listening to W. Edwards Deming. Along came Carol Dweck with her psychology research on growth mindset versus fixed mindset. It helped me see why Deming's idea was so powerful and also why it was difficult to explain. The audiences were in a fixed-mindset school trying to figure out how a growth-mindset process could fit. I had the practical knowledge from Deming and the psychology from Dweck. Then John Hattie sat down with me and shared how to use the scatter diagram that Deming taught to calculate effect sizes. Even further, Hattie's Visible Learning research proved why Deming's original idea actually worked. Now you are reading the synthesis of Deming, Dweck, and Hattie.

As educators we want to organize the learning environment so that students are using the surface-learning they have obtained for both synthesis and analysis deep learning.

The third aspect of Hattie's learning triangle, when divided into halves, is interdisciplinary learning and creativity. Interdisciplinary learning is most often led by adults and creativity is led by students.

Interdisciplinary instruction in elementary schools can be a full day on a single theme. When I was teaching university courses in elementary teaching methods, one of the assignments we gave future teachers was to take a topic they knew very well and use it as the organizer for a day with elementary-age students. The university students came up with geometry, measurement, statistics, history, geography, civics, science, literature, music, and art experiences tied to their interests. The organizing topics ranged from skiing to bicycling to soccer. It didn't matter what the interest was, university students found every subject buried inside their interest. Fun. This use of one of 180 days in a school year will not be forgotten.

For middle schools, interdisciplinary instruction often involves four teachers who share the same students: math, language arts, social studies, and science. It usually doesn't matter what the topic of the interdisciplinary unit is—there are connections for all four teachers. The interdisciplinary units usually last several weeks in the spring of the year.

I do not see this same structure working in high schools because of the scheduling.

However, there are ways to encourage interdisciplinary thinking for advancement of transfer learning. One is to state to all students, "You are encouraged to work with two or more of your teachers to complete one assignment and get credit from multiple teachers. In your student handbook is a form to fill out requesting permission from the participating teachers. The teachers will need to agree upon your proposal and have the same due date." Interdisciplinary learning can also be encouraged through a senior project or through an elective course with students creating a project much like the future teachers were assigned earlier in this chapter.

Creativity is when two or more known items are put together in an unusual or new way. Almost all inventions are created by such combinations. Students are always combing ideas from several sources into a new idea. These students need to hear from parents and teachers, "What a creative idea. How did you think of that?" The reason this is so important is that far too often creativity is thought of as occurring only in the arts. Wrong. Creativity is everywhere and all students need to hear the creativity compliment when they combine known items in a new way.

Similar to creativity is intuition. "It is getting ideas from the blue ... Our educational system fatally undervalues the role of intuition in intellectual and creative life. Many of the great discoveries came through the intuitive channels" (Thompson, 1995, p. 54).

All students want to think of themselves as smart. Educators using the LtoJ process make this desire come true in multiple ways every day. It starts with Part I, followed by the removal of the practices described in Part II that destroy the love of school learning. In Part III, educators learn how students can visibly see themselves as smart and getting smarter on a very regular basis.

Students thrive off knowing that they are smart, competent learners.

CHAPTER 18

Schools' Most Powerful Pair: Ears

"The number one job of leaders is to create more leaders."

W. Edwards Deming

The process of teach, assign homework, grade homework, and assess short-term memory on a chapter test is a failed education process. The replacement is teach, listen with eyes and ears to student feedback, lead the learning, assess long-term memory and celebrate. In order for decades of poor processes to be replaced, there has to be a new type of leadership inside of the classroom. This type of leadership empowers both teachers and students to take control of the education process to drive their own learning.

Leadership with a major emphasis upon listening is the focus of Part III of *How to Create a Perfect School*. The graphs are for listening for answers to the simple question, "Are we on track to meet end-of-year standards?" A quick glance at the class run chart can inform curious observers about the answers to the question. It is easy to see if the students have learned 25% of the content at the end of first quarter, 50% of the content by semester, 75% by third quarter, and then how close can we get to 100% before the year is over. The histogram, when standards are very high, will be in the shape of an *L* in the beginning of a school year. If the classroom is on a successful path, the histogram will be a bell midyear and then moving closer and closer to the right side of the graph. The *J* gradually appears as the final quarter comes to an end. This is the genesis of the name "LtoJ."

The scatter diagram, because it shows a dot for every student every quiz, provides a dramatic look at the marching of learning towards the upper right of the graph. It is amazing to me how many students state that this is their favorite graph. It must be because it displays both the class and individuals at the same time.

Instead of being fooled by chapter tests and relying upon state assessments that provide results long after the students have left, these three graphs all inform teachers about long-term memory quickly enough to make instructional adjustments before the end of the school year. A few more listening tools that connect to the graphing are explained in this chapter. These additional tools engage students in a way that improves learning for the whole class. These tools include:

1. It is guaranteed that all class run charts will have plateaus, where the graph seems to be stuck, not going up or down. When this happens, call a class meeting and solicit ideas for returning the graph to an upward trend. Students should provide hypotheses and then vote on one they most agree on. The teacher decides to test out this hypothesis for a period of three weeks or so. If it works, the class continues using the decided-upon method. If it does not work, then have another class meeting and start the process over. Amazingly, students generate ideas that the teachers never even think of trying. "Experience is not the very best teacher; the best way to learn is to continually test theories" (W. Edwards Deming). By allowing students to test different theories in order to continue to generate the growth of knowledge acquisition, teachers are putting this quotation to work and seeing wonderful results.

2. Item analysis of errors for the class is another listening device. Blank item analysis graphs are located at www.LBellJ.com. Figure 18.1 is a blank graph for a quiz with ten questions. It is usually started in the second quarter of the year. Teachers gather and organize the data in different ways, but the final result is a graph for students and teachers that depicts the most errors to the fewest errors (Figure 18.2). This graph is used to focus on which question is missed by the most students the most often. Very often a review question from prior grade levels is missed by

Fig. 18.1

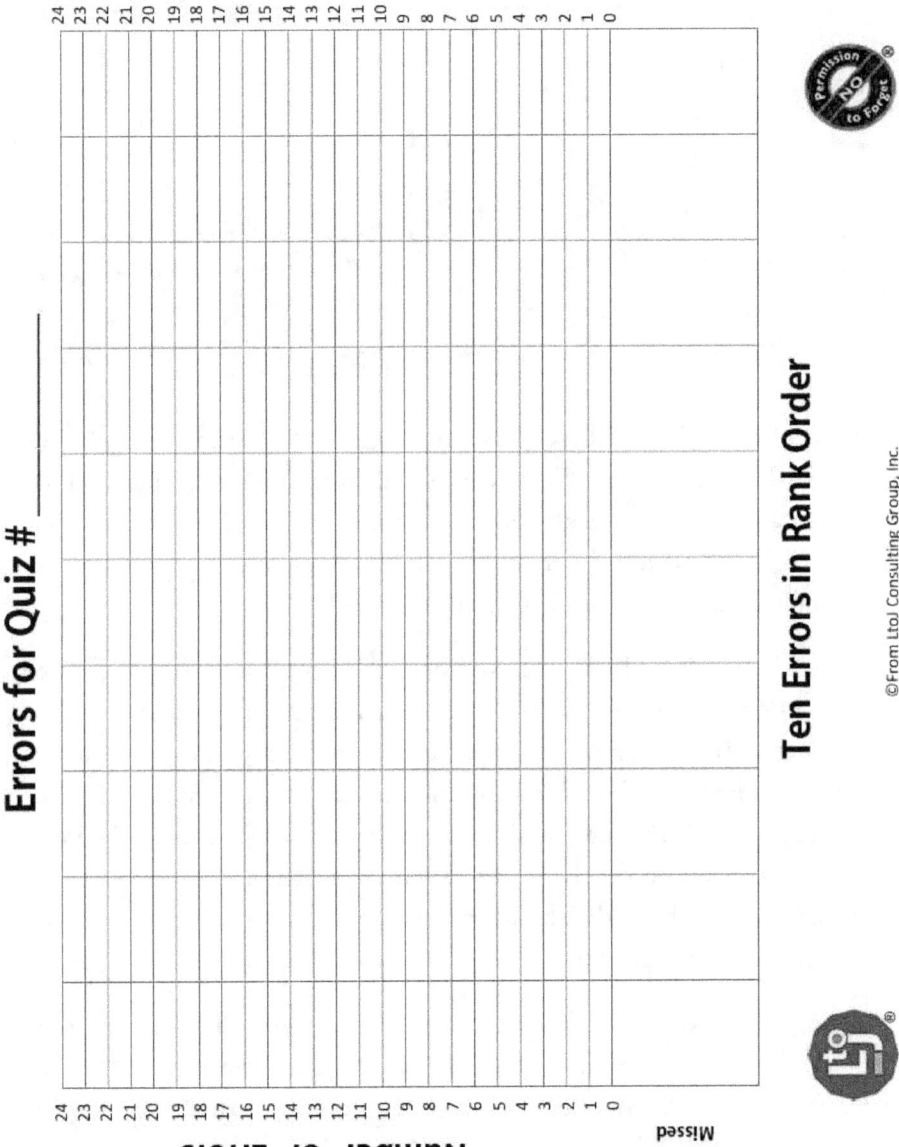

Errors for Quiz # _____

Number of Errors

Ten Errors in Rank Order

Most to Fewest Missed

©From LtoJ Consulting Group, Inc.

Fig. 18.2

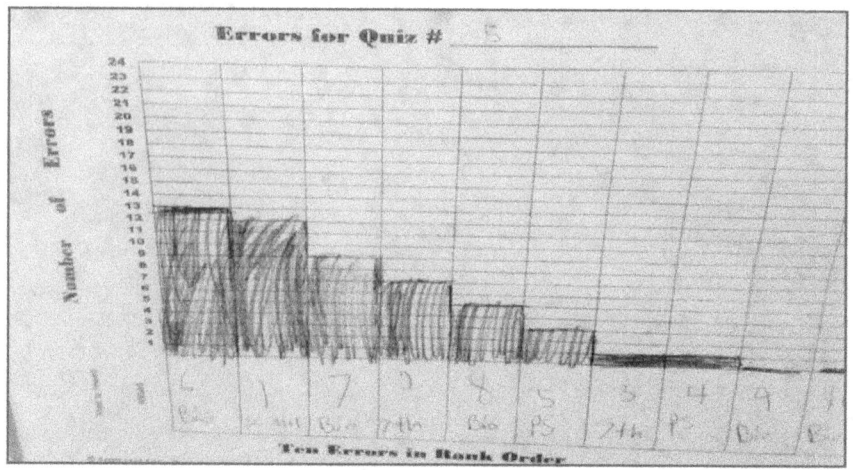

quite a few students. There are some surprises along the way, including times when most of the class correctly answers a preview question. By having a graph that quickly relates missed knowledge, teachers are able to correct and review the material before it becomes a distant memory and an unlearned concept left in the past.

3. In a high school biology class where the LtoJ questions were asked with a PowerPoint deck, I asked the students how the process could be improved. Their suggestion was to add sound and graphics to each of the slides. For a teacher, this suggestion is very easy to implement—the students provide the suggested sounds and graphics for each of the PowerPoint slides used for the quizzes. It may be that this only assists the students who submit the sound or the graphic, but a little improvement is improvement indeed.

4. After a quiz or any assignment is completed, the teacher can save time on scoring papers and also give students time to help each other. The teacher collects the completed assignments and scores them immediately in the classroom. While the teacher is scoring the papers, the students are put in groups of three to four and are asked to redo the assignment while agreeing upon the answers. Then each group must check with one other group and reach an agreement on the answers. When the teacher finishes

scoring the papers and the students finish redoing the assignment, the class goes over the answers as a whole. Because the groups had debates while repeating the assignment, there is a lot of listening occurring in the classroom. In one case the math problem was to calculate the perimeter of a rectangle. Two students calculated the perimeter and two the area. They wanted to know who was right. In another example, one of the questions for students was to circle the noun in the sentence, "We went to the skateboard park." Every group agreed that the noun was skateboard, but two students, who were outvoted, said the answer was park. Wonderful *a-has* and insightful classroom discussion ensued. The more students question and debate their answers, the more the learning is reinforced and subsequently, the material is reexplained, which cements the knowledge in students' minds.

I began this chapter with the sequence: teach, listen to student feedback, lead learning, assess long-term memory and celebrate. We now will continue with the celebrations of increased learning.

We often hear how wonderful it is when "students own their learning." It is true. A very exciting flip occurs in classrooms when the teacher no longer needs to pressure the students to learn more; the students are pressuring the teacher to teach more. Students are accepting much of the leadership responsibilities for their own learning. With this acceptance, students are more driven to learn, which creates even more excitement for teachers and thus parents and administrators.

One seemingly simple listening activity would be to ask, "Did we meet our goal?" This simplicity is damaged, however, by having fake goals. Assume a class has a total of 237 spelling words correct, and somebody says, "Our goal is now 250." That is a fake goal. Where did 250 come from? Why not 260? Why not 300? The real goal should be 238. Here is what happens when fake goals are not met: people do not know whether to be happy or sad. It is like receiving one message in the left ear and the opposite message in the right ear. In our example above, should a class have a fake goal of 250 and then score 243, they are sad. One ear hears they are dumb because they did not meet their goal. The other ear hears they are smart because they outperformed their prior best. We must remove this double hearing problem; both ears must hear the same thing. Remember, celebrating ATB is leadership and gratitude melted together.

There can also be annual goals; they are to outperform the prior year's data. Look at the class run chart in Chapter 15 from Angela Willnerd's classroom in Fremont, Nebraska. See the line across the graph at 243? That was her best score from prior years and this year's students surpassed 243 on quiz 23.

The charts are listening devices for students, teachers, and administrators. More interesting charts equals more opportunities for all to learn from the data. Fortunately, students like taking on these responsibilities. Allan Culp created two new jobs for students. The first is students keeping track, concept by concept, of the number of times each concept has been assessed over the course of the year. I have known teachers who kept this tally, but not students. The second is a histogram with data from all four of his periods of social studies. The first period of the day makes a histogram in the regular fashion. Then period two adds their data on top of first period, then third period and finally his fourth period. This histogram provides a clear picture of how all his classes are doing all together. What a beautiful *J* curve at the end of a school year!

Every leadership decision by teachers or administrators can demotivate students, maintain intrinsic motivation, or accelerate intrinsic motivation. The leadership decisions to (1) always visualize learning progress, (2) make adjustments based upon what the data say, (3) create collective student and staff efficacy based upon continued improvement, (4) engage students in decisions about their learning, and (5) always search for new, meaningful responsibilities for students are powerful in the present and in the future. The movement towards a more perfect school depends upon these decisions. LtoJ provides the very structure to make all five of these listening leadership actions possible.

CHAPTER 19

Parents Assist with Keeping the Dream Alive

"Your enthusiasm for the process of learning's sake is vital to instilling the same in your child."

Jessica Lahey

"It is startling to see the degree to which people with the fixed mindset do not believe in effort."

Carol Dweck

In *How to Create a Perfect School*, the role of parents, as they assist in the education of their children, takes a huge step forward. Instead of parents responding only to daily homework and projects due in a week or so, now parents know for the whole year the surface-learning their children are being taught. The purpose of this chapter is to provide ideas for parents regarding how to assist home learning with this big list. Remember, "Success is a derivative of persistence" (Batterson, 2014, 87). Cramming for a weekly quiz is fairly easy; helping students to learn and remember a whole year's content takes persistence. Parents see the end of the year better than their children.

As I write this, I cannot help but think of all the advertisements for medication; they all contain a warning. So, here is the warning for parents with the key-concept list for the whole year. Remember, it is for the *WHOLE* year. Please do not make this painful for children by insisting they learn a *WHOLE* year's content in a week or so. Let's enjoy the process for the year—students, parents, and teachers. Enjoyable ideas for the year follow:

1. Hopefully you have received a couple copies of the key-concept list. Cut one of the copies into strips—one key concept per strip. Place the strips into a container and randomly draw out one concept. One of you read the key concept. The child then states if the concept has been taught yet. If it is a review item, ask your child to tell you as much as they can remember. If it is a preview item, explain it to the child either from current knowledge or from looking on the internet.

2. Place a copy of the key concept list in the glove compartment of a family car. It will always be available for a conversation between a passenger and the student. If you want to select an item randomly, download a random number generator on a phone. It will be easy for the student to randomly select the number and the adult to lead a conversation with that item.

3. When students have their own phone, a new possibility is to text a key concept to your child with a word missing from the key concept. Ask your child to text back the correct word.

4. Even though key concepts are not trivia, every key concept has trivia connected to it. For example, when studying the 13 original US states, one might search out which state was first and why people were so anxious to be the first state.

5. Reverse roles: The job of the child is to teach parents about one of the key concepts at a designated time. Parents may either truly learn the new content or merely play the role of a student. Either way, this is fun.

6. Ask a grandparent if they have heard of_____.

7. Figure out what percentage of the school year has been used. Then figure out the percentage correct for the latest quiz. For

example, it might be the 45th day of the school year, which is 25% of the year. If a student takes 12-item LtoJ quizzes, how many were correct on the latest quiz? If the answer is four, the student had 33% correct compared to 25% of the time used. This is time for celebration; the child is ahead of expectations. This is the hardest adjustment parents have with the principles outlined in *How to Create a Perfect School*. Almost all education is based upon a goal of 100% correct for short-term memory. Now, students are being quizzed on long-term memory which we all know takes time. We cannot cram long-term memory into our heads; we must learn it over time.

8. Parent and child explore together the history of any item on the list. Assume *square root* is on the math key concept list. When was this invented? Why is it called square? Why is it called root? In English class, the teacher explains foreshadowing and asks students to use this literary device in an upcoming assignment. Who first used foreshadowing? What books use it?

9. Instead of asking, "What did you learn at school today?" say, "Let's look at your key-concept list and check off any new concepts taught today."

10. Quizzes can be made with PowerPoint very easily. Go to www.LBellJ.com under free resources/powerpoints. There are a lot of interesting PowerPoints created by teachers for LtoJ quizzes in their classrooms. The advantage of PowerPoint is that parents and students can change the questions/answers on the slides. The PowerPoint with the periodic table is particularly interesting. Change the questions/answers in any way you desire. (The editing to the slides is NOT done when in slideshow; it is done under the home tab.)

11. Go a step further than the previous suggestion and create your own PowerPoint for quizzes using hyperlinks. The format can be any area of interest to either parents or students. For

example, the first slide could be an automobile engine. Each part of the engine is linked to another slide with a question/answer. The process for using this PowerPoint deck for review could be to write each engine part on a popsicle stick or tongue depressor. Draw a stick, click on that part of the engine, and up will come a new slide with a question. Click on the spacebar and the answer you entered earlier will appear.

> **Traditional homework procedures actually create a lot of stress in households.**

Traditional homework procedures actually create a lot of stress in households. When parents have the list for the year, there is no deadline. Stress is replaced with joyful times between parents and their children. There is time to enjoy the learning and enjoy watching students grasp increasingly difficult concepts. As the author of this book, I am very interested in learning from families how they use the key-concept lists at home. Please send me an email at Lee@LBellJ.com with your story.

Parents, please remember that "Learning for many students is a risky business" (Hattie and Yates, 2014, p. 21). Children need parents who understand that there are "Two meanings to ability, not one: a fixed ability that needs to be proven, and a changeable ability that can be developed through learning" (Dweck,2009, 15). With the second definition, parents help children understand that a bad day at school is not permanent; it does not mean you are dumb; it only means that everyone has ups and downs. Let's look at the two extremes of parenting: at one end the child hears, "I knew you were no-good; you will never amount to anything." At the other extreme, the parent understands that grit is what we are after. "Gritty students succeed, and failure strengthens grit like no other crucible" (Lahey, 2015, p. XXI). This parental attitude reinforces the fact that effort pays off. We will have a fun celebration because our grit paid off.

Polishing Perfect

Persistence is probably the single most common quality of high achievers. They simply refuse to give up.

Jack Canfield

Why do so many promising ideas for education end up failing? It is often because prior to the introduction of the promising idea, the students' willingness to work hard is nonexistent and most students no longer receive any joy from school learning. At this point, an idea, any idea, falls on deaf ears.

Part IV includes systems that can increase student effort and joy in amazing ways. They have been proven successful in locales where students are not totally discouraged from a menu of imperfect practices.

When the imperfect practices are replaced with quality improvements and students are pressuring the teacher to teach more instead of the teacher pressuring the students to learn more, what are some of the systems that can be put in place to accelerate intrinsic motivation?

Because we all want as many high achievers as possible, Part IV will provide many, many ideas for you to implement in your environment.

There is no limit to what could be written for Part IV. Enough is included here to help educators and parents think of more perfect systems they can implement.

CHAPTER 20

If You Have a Better Idea, Come See Me

*People who hope to thrive in the Conceptual Age must understand the
connections between diverse, and seemingly separate, disciplines.
They must know how to like apparently unconnected
elements to create something new.*

Daniel Pink

Over the years I have read many education articles advocating student choice for their personal learning. Subsequently, I have been in thousands of classrooms and unfortunately choice is rarely visible. Why is there a disconnect?

Today's educators inherited an educational process that is not set up for choices. It is organized around chapters to be taught and pacing guides to ensure all chapters are at least "covered," if not taught. Teachers are expected to cover all of the information regardless of student interest or motivation. The same materials are expected to be used by all students regardless of their previous knowledge, abilities, and individual backgrounds. Choice, either by teachers or students, is not part of the system.

So how do we open up more choices for our students? Learning is enhanced when students have a voice regarding how they learn and thus an acceleration of intrinsic motivation occurs. "Joy in learning comes not so much from what is learned, but from the learning" (Deming, 1994, p. 145). In Part III, I discussed several methods used in the LtoJ process that gives students a voice and leading role in their own education. While they do not necessarily get to choose what they learn, they get to vocalize

Come visit our school district; the kids will explain it all to you.

how they want to learn. Using those methods to collect data, along with the following information regarding creative processes for accelerated learning, you will leave this book with the tools necessary to give your students choices and your teachers power to drive their learning.

The first structure is from Woody Wilson of West Virginia. His idea is profound—able to be used with all but the very youngest of students. He tells his students what they are expected to learn, gives them three ways they can prove to him they learned the content, and then states, "If you have another idea, come see me." One of his students completed almost every history assignment with political cartoons. She proved through the art that she comprehended the history. Angela Duckworth wrote, "I began to reflect on how smart even my weakest students sounded when they talked about things that genuinely interested them" (Duckworth, 2016, p. 17). By giving students a fourth option, Wilson taps into precisely what Duckworth wrote. The foundation for Wilson's process and all other ideas about choice I present in Chapter 20 are based on THE BIGGIE described in Chapter 13. Working off the key-concept list all year is crucial, as exemplified by Julie Otero. She wrote, "As an administrator I just love visiting classrooms to observe the results of Lee Jenkins' work. I see weekly everything he writes about in pre-kindergarten, elementary, middle and high school classrooms. The evidence is visible on charts and students' faces. Come visit our school district; the kids will explain it all to you."

Once the annual list of essential concepts is provided to every student, and the student-to-teacher LtoJ feedback process described in Part III is in place, who cares when or how students learn the essentials? It is only when the complete expectations for the year are presented that choice can become an everyday occurrence. As you read the ideas in the remainder of the chapter you will see that a structure is underneath each idea which makes implementation much simpler.

Ideas to try for enhancing student choice:

1. "My Important Word Book" for beginning readers: Each student has a book of blank paper and a cover entitled "My Important Word Book by____." Available in the classroom are stacks of blank flash cards. At a time when the whole class is not all working on the same assignment, a few students are asked the question, "What word would you like to learn to read?" The word is written on a flash card and on a page of the Important Word Book. The job of students is to write the word five times on a slate board, once in the word book, and then draw a picture of the word and either write or dictate a sentence to go with the word. Figure 20.1 shows a drawing by my youngest son, Jim, during his first week of kindergarten. Nobody knows why he wanted the word 'caveman.' All of the phonics students need to learn is naturally built into these words. At various times students will be asked to read their flash cards. They will know some, but not others. For a word they cannot read from the flashcard, they match the word on the flashcard with the word in their "My Important Word Book," and almost always can recognize the word from the picture.

Fig. 20.1

2. It is quite common to have journals or writing books in class-rooms. Instead of assigning a time for everyone to write in their journal, teachers can save the journal for times when a student is emotional about something. It can be a happy, sad, angry, or nervous emotion. The student then knows exactly what they want to write about. Two journal entries come to mind from previous students: (1) the student who had a birthday coming and hoped that her siblings would not get a present because it was *her* birthday and (2) the kindergartner whose house was burglarized. He wrote all the details he remembered, from the robbery to the police taking fingerprints.

3. At some grade level students are expected to understand gram weights. Most schools have balance scales with two empty buckets but do not have metric weights. These come in sets that include one kilogram, 500 gram, 250 gram, 100 gram, 50 gram and 10 gram weights and cost about $15. Instead of a unit on metric weight, all year long the center is available for students to choose what they want to weigh. Just about anything that is in the classroom is selected by some students to weigh. They hold a kilogram in their hand and know how much it weighs as they experience what no video or book can provide. The key concept of metric measurement is learned throughout the year, with choice being front and center. When each student has a Personal Math Book composed of blank paper, it is quite easy for them to write the date on the page and record the weight of everything they weighed.

4. Instead of having all of the rulers distributed one by one in individual desks, it may be wise to place them in one container. Students determine what they want to measure as illustrated in Figure 20.2. This student researched pythons and found that some are 30 feet long. She gathered up 30 rulers, placed them end to end, and then cut off a piece of yarn that was 30 feet long. Next, meter sticks were laid down adjacent to the

Fig. 20.2

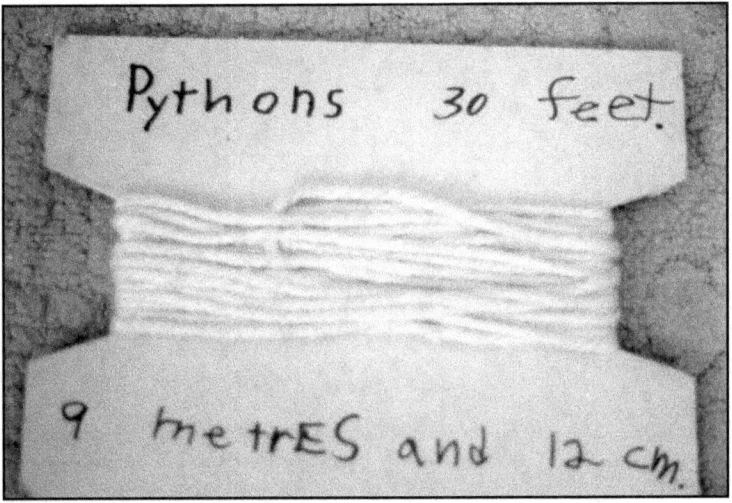

rulers and a second measurement was recorded on the precut cardboard. The classroom collection of lengths was often utilized at recess by various students to unwind and learn.

5. At all ages people enjoy making pictures with Pattern Blocks. Even so-called non- artists can create a recognizable picture with the Pattern Blocks. The picture is then reproduced with the Pattern Block template and is the basis for writing. It can be a nonfiction report or fiction; it doesn't matter. It is the choice about the picture and the joy of creating with the Pattern Blocks that makes this such a winning activity.

One summer my wife, Sandy, and I visited a number of East Coast historical sites. We purchased 32-page picture books over the course of the trip. Sandy read the books over the course of the year with her Grade 3 students and they created art and writing based upon a special memory of hearing the book read. Figure 20.3 is an example of a Pattern Block/Pattern Block Template picture.

Fig. 20.3

This is a minuteman. He is by the Bridge That the red coats are going to come on. He is all ready

6. On the internet one can find multiple tangram pictures. Each of them is made with the seven tangram pieces. The choice activity here is for students to look through a collection of a dozen tangram pictures and pick out which one they want to write about. The student then solves the geometry problem, draws the tangram picture over using a tangram template and writes about the chosen picture. In the process, the tangram picture is often embellished with background and other features. The Paul Revere tangram story is from the same

Fig. 20.4

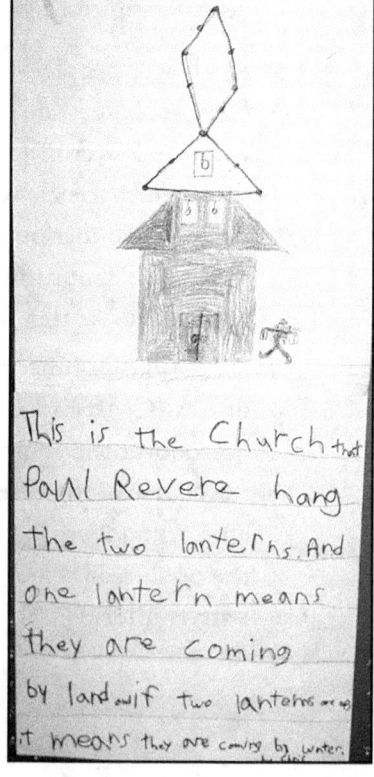

This is the Church that Paul Revere hang the two lanterns. And one lantern means they are coming by land, if two lanterns it means they are coming by water.

process as described earlier with the Pattern Blocks except that the dozen or so tangram puzzles were selected with Paul Revere in mind.

7. We want students to know the parts of speech, contractions, and other important concepts in language arts. The printed materials usually provided to teachers rarely give any choices to students. One solution is to provide blank booklets titled, for example, "My Book of Compound Words." Students receive a cover, a blank book with space for the word, a circle for the art, and room for a sentence or two. The back cover is usually a more traditional set of questions. One could say the back cover is a "left-brain" activity and the interior of the booklet is "right-brain." Students are able to select their own compound words instead of the ones selected by an adult editor. These words will hold a special meaning for students, which will help them remember the words and the usage. Other titles

Fig. 20.5

Inside pages for My Books of _____

Fig. 20.6

My Book of Compound Words

Name
School
Teacher
Date

Combine these words to create six new compound words:

pop	rain	ball
water	under	bow
play	wear	corn
base	ground	melon

1. _____
2. _____
3. _____
4. _____
5. _____
6. _____

Sample Cover

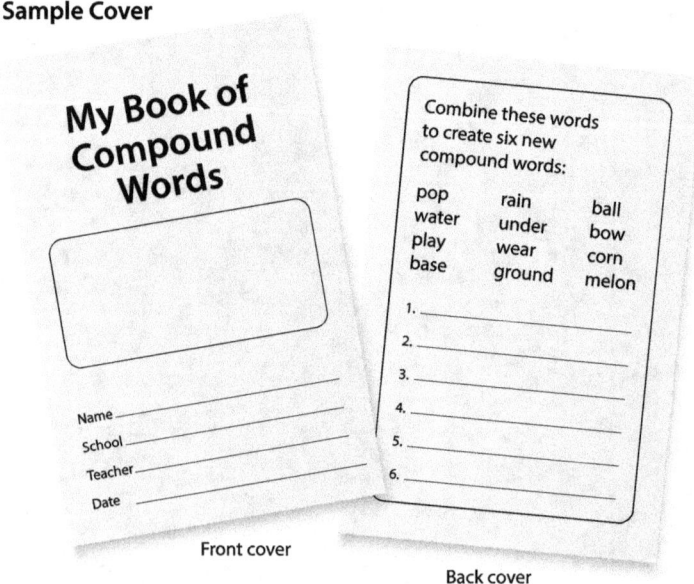

Front cover

Back cover

could include the examples below. In addition other sample book covers are located on the *How to Create a Perfect School* resource files under chapter 20. See www.LBellJ.com/perfect.

My Book of Similes

My Book of Quotations

My Book of Plurals Other than S

My Book of Verbs

My Book of Adjectives

My Book of Antonyms

8. My Dictionary. For this choice assignment, students are assigned to write a dictionary of 10 or so words. It works best when there is one word per page so at the end the pages can be alphabetized with a cover. Students will write dictionaries such as:

My Baseball Dictionary

My Bug Dictionary

My Space Dictionary

My Dog Dictionary

My Computer Dictionary

My Bicycle Dictionary

My Car Dictionary

Students look in a real dictionary to see what is included. Each of the words they select must indicate what part of speech it is and include a definition, a phonetic pronunciation, a sentence, and a picture. There may also be idioms, synonyms, and antonyms.

9. Our Classroom Encyclopedia. Even though since the advent of the internet encyclopedias are minimally used, this choice idea works well. Every classroom has students who are experts in some topic. Perhaps they learned all about bees from a

grandparent. Teachers run across this information all the time, but they rarely know what to do with this expertise. One way to capture this student knowledge is to have students write about their area of extensive knowledge. The students type up their encyclopedia entry, print a copy to take home and one to go into the three-ring binder "encyclopedia" in the classroom. It has alphabetic dividers and entries from multiple years.

10. ABC Books are wonderful for student choices at all grade levels. As one would expect, the most sophisticated one I have seen is *The ABC Book of Welding*, created by a high-school agriculture student. ABC books can be for the classroom unit reflection or for individual reports. When it is to be used in the classroom, each student submits one page as a way to look back at a recently completed unit. The *ABC Book of Lewis and Clark* and *ABC Book of Ancient Egypt* are examples of classroom books. The *ABC Book of Math Vocabulary* is an example of a middle school individual assignment.

    When creating these books be sure not to insist that all pages begin with the designated letter. For example, in the *ABC Book of Ancient Egypt, X* is for Sphinx. In the *ABC Book of Math, J* is for adjacent. The art and writing requirements are to be adjusted according to the age of the students. In a kindergarten class's *ABC Book of Occupations*, the *Y* page is Y is for Yoyo Maker, plus a picture. For kindergartners this is enough. For older students the writing becomes much more detailed.

11. It is certainly acceptable for all students to read and discuss the same novel. However, the assignment for individual students should be to compare elements of the novel to another book of their choice. Students cannot go into Barnes and Noble and find the answers to this assignment. The computerized programs for reading may have their place, but they cannot handle student choice, comparison, and justification of answers.

It is always a good idea for teachers at all grade levels to tell students, "Please give me ideas regarding how you can learn the key concepts on your list. I may not be able to adjust to incorporate your

the leaders are not supposed to have all of the good ideas.

idea, but I promise you that I will listen. I will not immediately say 'No' to your suggestion, but I will give it some thought. The purpose here is for you to learn; how you learn is not nearly as important as that you do learn. When I prepared the list, I removed everything that might be nice to know and included only what I consider essential. So, your ideas are crucial." Teachers are the leaders of the learning, but just like any boss of any company, the leaders are not supposed to have all of the good ideas. When students provide the idea for a choice and then carry it out, we have gone a long way towards polishing perfect.

CHAPTER 21

Raise Your Hand if You Are Impressed with Commercial Posters in Classrooms

We must strive for a natural, human, democratic relationship. This means involving students from the beginning in creating the environment. They must help in decision-making about the physical setting.

Canfield and Wells, 1976

Please, please, administrators: Tell your staff how unimpressed you are by adult work displayed on classroom walls. You especially need to tell your newly credentialed, newly hired teachers. It is almost certain that they will be organizing their classroom for their first class of students prior to receiving their first paycheck. More credit card debt on top of student loans is not a positive way to start a career. You can encourage these teachers and the rest of your staff to create a welcoming classroom environment without the use of cheesy slogans and outdated posters.

The classroom walls are for displaying student work. This includes the ABCs above the white board, every bulletin board, every closet door that can double as a bulletin board, and the hallway outside the room. The exceptions that come to mind are maps and emergency information. Maybe there are other adult-created items to place on the walls, but they are few.

If a collection of small posters is already posted, I would leave them. However, one by one these can be gradually replaced by student work. The wording may be similar, but the art will be student original work. The alphabet above the white board is an example. If it is already in place, leave it until one by one the letters, words, and pictures are replaced. I do suggest using a letter cutter, such as manufactured by Ellison, to cut out the capital and lower-case letters.

The classroom walls are for displaying student work.

Beyond that, the choice of words and pictures should be up to students. In many places the alphabet letters come from the publisher of the reading textbook and teachers are instructed not to replace these adult-created posters. I would encourage educators to realize that student ownership of the room environment is a higher priority than the advice of a textbook publisher.

If certain sounds are on the commercial posters, this can be improved upon by having multiple student-created alphabet posters for each letter. Because there is no letter in English that is always pronounced the same way, classrooms can have created letter posters galore. Some letters, when pronounced, are always pronounced the same. However, many times these letters are silent. The alphabet above the white board could be for only words where the letter sound is heard. A separate place in the room can be created to display silent letter words. The letter C, as an example, can be used with the word 'science.' I am not trying to overload beginning readers with phonetic-sound posters. What I have in mind is another structure to engage students in classroom ownership. When a student comes across the word 'science' and learns that the *c* is silent, it will be easy for the teacher to suggest that the student add it to the silent letter collection.

Often there are rules posted in LtoJ classrooms. In many cases, these have been created by the students. What is often missing are the rules for the teacher. Students and teachers can engage in a discussion about what the expectations are for both parties. These two lists should be posted side by side in the classroom. Students and teachers are more likely to follow rules and structures when they are part of the process of creating and posting their own expectations.

Student writing is the number-one item to display in classrooms. Ideally, the art and the writing are combined into one display. Something is wrong when the art is displayed on one wall and the writing is nowhere near. It is often during the creation of the art that students come up with the basic idea for their writing. Further, it is the art that attracts people to the writing. With younger students the art should always come first, followed by the writing. As students progress through intermediate grades and beyond, more and more students become sensitive about their artistic ability. Every teacher can always state, "For all writing assignments, everyone always has permission to draw first and write second." These students always seem to think better about their writing while drawing. Authors who create picture books for students seem to be equally divided between those who think first through art and those who think first with written language.

Remember, visuals can be created in many ways. This is especially true today with all of the apps students have available on their phones.

This chapter, while focusing upon the wall space thus far, is really about student ownership of the classroom space. What decisions should the students be involved in? Below are a few:

1. The location for direct instruction. Every student in their own desk is not the only structure. Ask students where they want to sit or stand when you are teaching a lesson. Some will sit on the floor, others sit on the desk, some will sit in a desk, and some will stand. There may be some competition to sit in the teacher's chair.

2. Once students help arrange the room space for direct instruction, there is far more flexibility with regard to the organization of the rest of the classroom. The rest of the room becomes workspace. Not all chairs, for example, are facing the front of the room, because this is workspace, not a place to sit and listen to instruction.

3. Students can be involved with storage locations for nonelectronic materials and electronic equipment.

4. Where are the graphs described in Parts I and III going to be posted?

5. Do we need lamps? Other furniture? Music? A small fountain for soothing sounds during work time?

6. Using a trellis as a room divider might be a good idea. Would they like it? Would it be helpful?

As stated earlier, it is the creation of the key-concept list that is the foundation for choices in Chapter 20 and student involvement in the learning environment in Chapter 21. It is the stress teachers and administrators feel for higher test scores that often makes schools so rigid. When the key-concept list is the guide for the year and the evidence is posted that students are on track to learn all of the content, as explained in Part III, teachers have the mindset to relax and give students choices for both assignments and room environment.

CHAPTER 22

Hearing Aids for Teachers

Good leaders motivate others by their listening skills.

John Maxwell

W. Edwards Deming stated that feedback was from customers and evaluation from bosses. We do not usually think of students as customers, so for our purposes we will change the statement for parents and educators. Feedback for a teacher comes from parents and students; evaluation comes from the principal. Feedback for the principal comes from parents, students, teachers, and support staff; evaluation comes from the superintendent or a designee. Feedback for the superintendent comes from parents, teachers, principals, other administrators, and community members; evaluation comes from the school board.

Merriam-Webster defines feedback as "the transmission of evaluative or corrective information about an action, event, or process to the original or controlling source." Such information could also be referred to as a listening device. In the school system, all of these devices are time sensitive, which means the feedback must come to the teacher in time to make adjustments before the end of the school year. There is certainly value in end-of-year feedback as teachers plan for the next year. However, ideally, adjustments should be made midyear. Kramer writes, "Because listening is such an important component in today's world, leading-edge companies are creating their own listening systems and dedicated teams to run them (Kramer, 2016, p. 70). It seems businesses and public institutions all need formal listening devices. Our schools need to take a lesson from these companies and learn how to listen and respond to feedback for the sake of our students, their customers.

"I realized that the most powerful single influence enhancing achievement is feedback ... it dawned upon me that the most important feature was the creation of situations in classrooms for the teachers to receive more feedback about their teaching—and then the ripple effect back to the student was high" (Hattie, 2009, p. 12). Using Hattie's knowledge, I knew that our education professionals needed help creating timely feedback systems.

In *How to Create a Perfect School* you have already been introduced to the following listening devices:

Chapter 3: The Will & Thrill Matrix and Feedback Form

Chapter 4: The Social-Circle Survey

Chapter 14: The Student Run Chart

Chapter 15: The Classroom Graphs (class run chart, scatter diagram, histogram)

The class run chart is instrumental to classrooms because teachers can comprehend at a glance if their students are on track to meet end-of-year standards. Is the class demonstrating knowledge of at least 25% of the surface-learning at the end of first quarter? 50% by semester, 75% by third quarter, and is the class very, very close to 100% at the end of the school year? A quick glance at the chart and the answers are right in front of the teachers and students. No need to wonder what the test scores will reveal, or if there will be any surprises at the end of the year. No more wondering, and no more abstract assumptions. The evidence hangs on the wall for all to witness the growth of individuals on the scatter diagram and the class, as a whole, on the class run chart.

A number of people, including Will Black, the assistant superintendent of schools in Paducah, Kentucky, urged me to show John Hattie my work that I described in Part III. So, at Corwin's Visible Learning Conference outside Washington D.C. in 2016, I was determined to take this advice. At the end of the conference I showed Hattie slides from classrooms utilizing LtoJ. When we came to the scatter diagram, he said, "Lee, everything you need to calculate effect size is included in that chart." I was surprised—I thought that effect size was far too complicated. Since that time, the LtoJ Effect-Size Calculator, created by Jason Gain, the LtoJ IT Manager, has become a very powerful listening device for teachers. It provides teachers and students data every quarter that allows them to compare the learning in their classroom to the average of 250 other influences upon learning. The research is located at VisibleLearningPlus.com. Click on the research tab and then download the two-page pdf for the research.

The data for the LtoJ Effect-Size Calculator are located on the classroom scatter diagram.

On the scatter diagram, the first three columns are shaded. This is the base-line data. Next, the last three quizzes each quarter are shaded. The calculator then provides an effect size comparing the most recent quarter's entry to the first three quizzes. Teachers and students can see instantly if their work equals an average influence upon learning, double the average, or even up to 10 times the average learning.

The effect-size calculator looks like this: Directions for obtaining the LtoJ Effect-Size Calculator are available at LBellJ/perfect.

The numerals you see represent the dots on the scatter diagram. For example, if on the first quiz there were three 0s, four 1s, one 2, etc., then the effect size calculator for quiz 1 would start like this:

0
0
0
1
1
1
1
2

A constant thread of thought throughout *How to Create a Perfect School* is preserving intrinsic motivation instead of giving students a constant barrage of extrinsic motivators.

Education has no shortage of prizes, incentives, and parties to extrinsically motivate students. What education lacks are multiple ways to celebrate learning with real evidence. The annual test-score reports that come from the various state departments of education several months after the school year is over are totally inadequate. The LtoJ Effect-Size Calculator provides accurate, real data quarterly. Teachers and students are often celebrating at the end of the first quarter because they have already learned the same amount of information as the average classroom learns in a year. Instead of bribing students to complete tasks, the students realize how much they have learned already and know their hard work has paid off. The effect-size calculator is a hearing aid for teachers and students regarding how much has been learned; the subsequent celebration is a result of the learning.

I was invited into Allan Culp's Grade 7 history class because the effect size had gone down. The effect-size calculator displayed the baseline data from the first three quizzes and then the effect size at the end of the first three quarters. At the end of the first quarter, students were very pleased with more than a year's learning already. At the end of the

> **They admitted to each other that they had become complacent, prideful, and lazy.**

semester their effect size was already four times the average for a whole year. However, the effect size went down for the third quarter. Allan asked his Grade 7 students the simple question, "What happened?" They admitted to each other that they had become complacent, prideful, and lazy. The effect size was a wake-up call the students did not like. The year ended with an effect size of 5.30, which is 13 times the average effect size. There was no way these students were going to end the year with a negative trend!

In *Optimize Your School* I included a survey for teachers to ask their students to anonymously fill out. This document, influenced by prior work of Vic Cottrell, has statements such as, "When things go crazy, my teacher is calm . . . always, sometimes, or never." The results from this survey are not evaluations to be shared with the principal (unless desired by the teacher). They are feedback for the teacher to ponder and make suggestions. The teacher can then ask for advice to improve a less desirable habit and celebrate for feedback regarding an exemplary habit.

Students have amazing solutions. Nothing has impressed me more than student solutions to learning problems. In Chapter 15 you read about the class run chart, which is merely the total correct for the whole class. I guarantee that this graph will flatline someday. It won't be going up or down; it will appear stuck. Flatlines create the urgency necessary to ask students for hypotheses to test in order to help the class run chart return to an upward trajectory. Students brainstorm ideas for what members of the class can try. They are not to brainstorm on what students can do at home; this needs to be what the students can do together. The ideas are written on the whiteboard and then students vote on what idea they like the best or believe will be of the most help to them. An agreement is reached with the teacher regarding how much class time can be allocated for testing out their idea. Three weeks is sufficient time to test out a hypothesis. If the graph has not gone up by then, a new class meeting needs to be held and a new hypothesis agreed upon for testing during the next three weeks. If the original idea worked, there is no reason to stop using it until its usefulness is over. The graph will inform everyone when its time is finished. Another flatline means another classroom meeting and a new hypothesis to test. With this method, students and teachers are constantly engaging in active evaluations and, yes, feedback about what is and is not working. The best part is that feedback does not go to waste. If something ceases to work for learning, it ceases to be used as a method, and a new, more effective tool or procedure takes its place.

When students establish the hypothesis to test there is amazing curiosity on their part. They want to know if their idea improved the class learning. (Can we say the students want to know if their ideas were better than the teacher's ideas?) I estimate that 75% of the time the students' hypotheses do increase learning. An example of one such idea was provided by Grade 5 students regarding vocabulary. They suggested that the classroom play the game Heads Up, Seven Up more often. Their idea was that each time the teacher called on someone to guess who had touched their thumb, they were asked to define one of their vocabulary words. If their definition was correct, they were given two guesses and if the definition was incorrect, they received one guess. It worked.

An example of a hypothesis that did not work came from a middle school. The hypothesis was that if students could sit anywhere in the classroom they wanted, the learning would increase and be shown on the class run chart. After three weeks of no improvement, the students realized their hypothesis did not work and a new hypothesis was established. Instead of the teacher immediately shutting down the idea, the students' hypothesis is valued. Even though it did not work, the teacher listened to the feedback and made space for honoring student input.

The dichotomous rubric below further connects Chapter 15 with listening devices. We all know that our personal intrinsic motivation is not maintained when we are in an environment where our ideas and voices are not valued. Likewise, when our ideas are accepted, we are led to work even harder. As you look at the rubric, you will see that a yes to the final question really does add to the polish on perfect. John Maxwell is correct that good leaders motivate others with their listening skills.

Educators know this but need help with the tools to accomplish what they know, and thus Chapter 22 was written.

Graph Flatlined — Now What?

The Class Run Chart is Stuck!

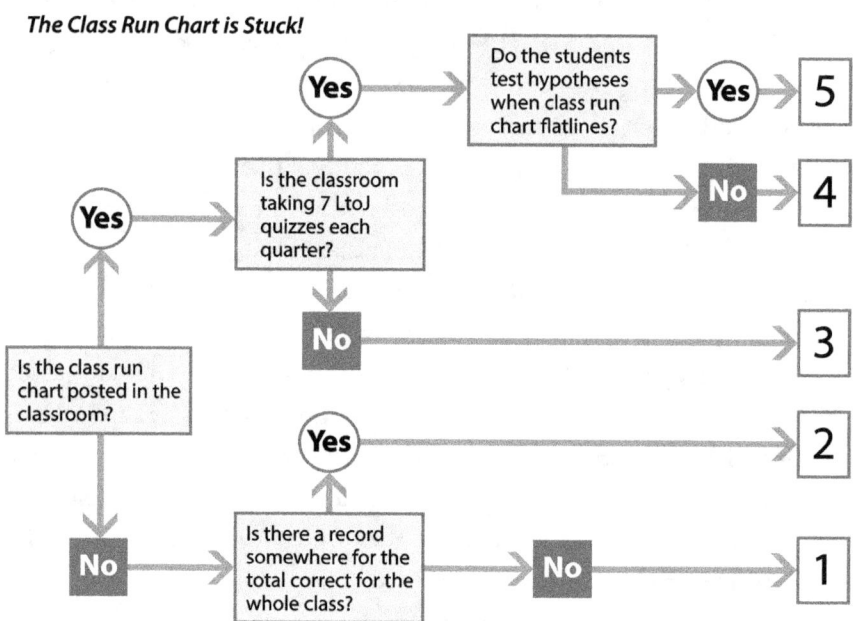

CHAPTER 23

Square Root Joy:
Cube Roots Anybody?

*"A content-neutral, skills-oriented concept of education has the
unintended effect of depressing reading scores and diminishing
the shared content we all need for communication and
solidarity within the nation as a whole."*

E.D. Hirsch

Polishing Perfect requires teaching with patterns as the foundation for understanding. Square roots are a good example of instruction organized upon patterns. The first step, which can be assignments in Grade 1 Personal Math Books, is this series of square root questions:

$$\sqrt{4} =$$
$$\sqrt{9} =$$
$$\sqrt{16} =$$
$$\sqrt{25} =$$
$$\sqrt{100} =$$
$$\sqrt{121} =$$
$$\sqrt{144} =$$
$$\sqrt{441} =$$

Obviously, this is not a normal first grade assignment. However, every time I have worked with first grade students on this task, they love it and are anxious to tell their parents. The prerequisite knowledge students need prior to being assigned square roots is knowledge of how to use

Base Ten Blocks. The direction to the students is to have them make squares with the base-10 blocks. The answer to the problem is the length of the sides. The most difficult problem above is $\sqrt{25} =$ because students need to place 25 blocks into a square. Much simpler is $\sqrt{441} =$, which only requires placing nine blocks in a square. Students learn early in their education that square roots are about squares; they are not learning about rectangle roots, hexagon roots, or triangle roots. The square root is simply the length of the sides of a square. So far there is no pattern with these problems. This now changes with this sequence of problems:

$$\sqrt{10} =$$
$$\sqrt{11} =$$
$$\sqrt{12} =$$
$$\sqrt{13} =$$
$$\sqrt{14} =$$
$$\sqrt{15} =$$
$$\sqrt{16} =$$
$$\sqrt{17} =$$
$$\sqrt{18} =$$
$$\sqrt{30} =$$
$$\sqrt{102} =$$
$$\sqrt{110} =$$
$$\sqrt{125} =$$

The Grade 5 students, starting with $\sqrt{10} =$, are told to personify the base-10 blocks. Pretend you are a 3 x 3 square, but you have always desired to become a 4 x 4 square. How many more blocks do you need to accumulate to become a 4 x 4 square? The answer is seven more blocks. Thus, if I have 10 blocks, I have a 3 x 3 square plus one block on my journey to obtain seven more blocks. The square root of 10 is approximately 3 1/7 because with 10 blocks I can make a 3 x 3 square plus I have 1/7 of the blocks I need to become a 4 x 4 square. The square root of 11 is 3 2/7. The square root of 12 is 3 3/7 and so on.

Fig. 23.1

√11≈3 2/7

Fig. 23.2

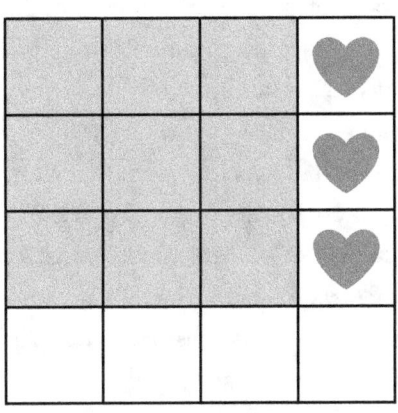

√12≈3 3/7

Students soon see the pattern and quickly answer the square-root problems up to the square root of 16 equals 4. Then comes the square root of 17. The personification exercise is to think, "I am now a 4 x 4 square and my new aspiration is to become a 5 x 5 square. Since I am a 4 x 4 square now, I need nine more blocks to become a 5 x 5 square. I need four blocks on the width, four blocks on the length and then one more in the corner. Thus, the square root of 17 is approximately 4 1/9. Students would write their answer as √17 ≈ 4 1/9. Because of calculators and computers, students no longer need to know how to calculate a precise decimal square root. However, they do need to know how to approximate the answer, and this geometric pattern process provides a very accurate approximation. An extension for this assignment is for students to use their calculator to obtain the precise square root and then to use the calculator to change the approximate square root into a decimal. For example, the actual square root of 17 is 4.1231. The decimal equivalent of 1/9 is .1111. The square root approximation is 4.111, when the actual square root is 4.1231, for a difference of .012. The difference between the approximation and the actual square root is minimal.

My purpose in writing the opening aspect of this chapter is to explore the power of patterns in human learning. I assume most readers of this book have been taught the formulas for estimating or calculating square roots. It probably was not a pleasant experience for the teacher or the students. Patterns make learning so much simpler. This is true at all ages and for all subjects. If you are fascinated by this square-root example, how about cube roots? Hang in there. If you have 10 blocks you can make a 2 x 2 x 2 cube and have two blocks left over. Your aim is to become a 3 x 3 x 3 cube. How many more blocks does a 2 x 2 x 2 cube need in order to become a 3 x 3 x 3 cube? It needs 19 more blocks. The cube root of 10 is approximately 2 and 2/19 because with ten blocks you can build a 2 x 2 x 2 cube and have 2/19 of the blocks necessary to build a 3 x 3 x 3 cube. What is the cube root of 1005? With base-10 blocks this a fairly easy question for students in intermediate and middle grades.

Readers know that typical textbook explanations, for far too much of education, include (1) the rule to learn, (2) an example problem, and (3) multiple random practice problems. Rarely are the problems organized into a pattern. In order to keep the intrinsic motivation at a kindergarten level of effort and joy, patterns are needed as the initial point of introduction to almost any topic. Continuing with mathematics, students learn math by counting. They can count in five-minute intervals to five or more hours, for example.

> 5 minutes
> 10 minutes
> 15 minutes = 1/4 hour
> 20 minutes

25 minutes
30 minutes = ½ hour
35 minutes
40 minutes
45 minutes = ¾ hour
50 minutes
55 minutes
60 minutes = 1 hour
65 minutes = 1 hour and 5 minutes
70 minutes = 1 hour and 10 minutes
75 minutes = 1 ¼ hour
80 minutes = 1 hour and 20 minutes

This seems so boring to adults because we know the pattern. I have taught the square-root and cube-root pattern to many adults and they were not bored, because it was new information they wished had been explained years ago. Today's students are not bored by pattern assignments, because they experience great joy when they understand. Count by fractions to 10, count by cups to five gallons, by four-hour segments until you have a week, and so on. I suggest taking the 30° brown rhombus out of the Pattern Blocks and inform students that this is 30 degrees. Then count by degrees, gradually making a complete circle with the rhombuses. Two of the rhombuses make a 60° angle, three of them make 90°, and so on until we reach 360° and a complete circle.

The instructional design of starting with patterns for all grade levels is shown in the example below. The directions to the students are to graph the following equations:

$y=x+1$	$y=-x+2$	$y=4x+1$
$y=x+2$	$y=-x+3$	$y=-2x+1$
$y=x+3$	$y=-x+4$	$y=-3x+1$
$y=x+4$	$y=-x+5$	$y=-4x+1$
$y=x+5$	$y=2x+1$	$y=-5x+1$
$y=-x+1$	$y=3x+1$	

After learning through patterns, students are ready for the random problems provided in most textbooks and educational software. While writing this chapter, I received a phone call from a former Grade 5 student of mine, whom I taught in 1968. Susan Owens Delucchi recalled that through counting she came to understand fractions. She counted by 1/2s, 1/3s, 1/4s, and so on all the way to 10. The assignment was to write 1/3, 2/3, 3/3 = 1, 4/3 = 1 1/3, 5/3 = 1 2/3, 6/3 = 2, etc. Many readers will think, "There's not time for such an assignment." My response is, "Fractions are taught as a unit in every grade from kindergarten through Grade 8, and still the high school teachers wish they had students who truly understood fractions. A lot of time is spent teaching and reteaching rules that are not sticking."

In the United States we have three approaches to reading: sound, word, and sentence. Throughout the history of the United States, the country has switched approaches every few years. Each of the three approaches write stories for young readers that make success more likely. The sound approach limits words to those with short vowel sounds, for example. The word approach only uses previously taught words plus two new ones for the day's story. The sentence approach uses patterned language. Probably the best known of the sentence approach books for reading is Bill Martin, Jr.'s *Brown Bear, Brown Bear*. Readers might still be able to find copies of his collection of 30 Instant Readers—each book being based upon a pattern. One of my favorites is *Silly Goose and the Holidays* by Annabelle Sumera and adapted by Bill Martin, Jr.

The pattern is:

"Happy Thanksgiving, everyone!
No, no, Silly Goose! It's not Thanksgiving! It's Halloween! Oh, mercy me! So it is!
Merry Christmas, everyone!
No, no, Silly Goose!" And on goes the book through a whole year of holidays.

I choose not to participate in the "reading wars," arguing which of the three approaches is best. What I do know is that none of the three approaches works for every student and that some children may struggle with reading no matter which approach is utilized. I do not even argue with research showing that the sound approach has the best results. However, the sound approach does not create 100% success. There are some students in every school who need the patterns of the sentence approach or the word-by-word learning of the word approach to unlock the secret to reading print. Bill Martin, Jr. used the descriptor "Chunking" instead of "sentence approach."

This focuses upon clustering of words. He wrote about what he called an unnatural technique such as:

"insisting on paragraph forms
with rigid right-left hand margins that ignore
the natural grouping of words within a sentence" (Martin, 1972).

Teachers need the opportunity to teach each of these three methods to the students who need it, without worrying about getting in trouble for not using the approved method. Each student should receive the help they need to learn the pattern in whichever way makes the most sense.

It seems that every time I am really confused about something, it is because I do not see the pattern. I learn a few concepts, realize I understand, at the most, 5% of the topic, and give up. Once I see the pattern, I can fit more concepts into place and begin to build a more complete understanding in my mind. Continually, when students are frustrated in school it is due to a lack of understanding of the basic patterns of the topic currently being studied.

Continuing with language arts beyond beginning reading, there are always two constants: words and literature. Both have many, many patterns. I suggest readers look at sites like http://fun-with-words.com/ for word patterns and https://www.slideshare.net/CarverLangArts/recognizing-patterns-in-literature for patterns in literature. Let's help students see the word patterns and the literature patterns prior to delving into the more complex, deeper understanding of words and literature.

How many times have we all heard "history repeats itself?" I assume this is true, meaning that there are patterns in world history. Note that I wrote patterns in the plural; there are multiple patterns. It is my hypothesis that when history teachers share patterns in history with their students, it will give the students one more way of remembering the significant events being taught.

Here is a stab at a pattern: The first United States Congress had a big debate over slavery. One congressman, Elbridge Gerry, suggested that the United States use proceeds from sales of land in the West to pay slave owners for their slaves, thus compensating slave owners for what they (unfortunately) considered property they had purchased (Bordewich, 2016, 202). His suggestion was ignored. "Gerry had just broached the only policy that might peacefully have freed the nation's slaves and forestalled civil war, but it fell upon deaf ears." Consequently, we all know what occurred when Abraham Lincoln was President of the United States and the results of the Civil War. Could one of the historical patterns that always repeats itself in history be that (1) everyone recognizes there is a huge difference of opinion, (2) the solutions proposed are ignored, (3) the problem is set aside, and (4) future generations pay the price through a huge conflict?

Another pattern in history is that society expects that some huge investment of government funds or the work of some renowned expert will solve a problem. Then along comes an unknown person with the solution. Such was the case with the invention of the airplane by Orville and Wilbur Wright. The story is masterfully told by David McCullough in his book *The Wright Brothers*. He not only recounts the efforts of the two brothers, but details the United States government's funding of various experiments to develop some type of flying machine. It took officials, and society at large, extra time to accept the invention created by two unknowns. Pattern.

Allan Culp sent me a list of other history patterns to explore: (1) Conflict, Resistance, Change; (2) Identity Groups; and (3) Perseverance. Each of these have multiple examples from history. Perseverance examples are slaves, the underground railroad, women's rights/suffrage, immigrants, the Great Depression, 9/11, colonists, revolution, and Abraham Lincoln.

Science patterns are everywhere. Jeff Burgard shared that one of his students' favorite patterns involves ice changing to water and then changing to steam. They discover through experimenting that "temperature does not change while the substance is undergoing a phase change, but rises rapidly between changes. In other words, while ice is melting, the temperature stays constant, but as soon as it is all liquid, the temperature rises rapidly until the water boils. When the water boils, the temperature one again stays steady until it is all steam."

Debi (Mo) Walters wrote, "When I'm teaching my biomimicry course, we spend time in nature looking for patterns. Teaching the students about the mathematical patterns of Fibonacci which leads to fractals just blows their mind. We look at the Fibonacci sequence of a seashell, all the way to the depths of a spiral galaxy. We look at the human body, artichokes, pinecones and broccoli. Then we move onto the Sonoran desert looking at the patterns of flowing water and the blowing of sand dunes. The branching patterns occur very similar to what you find within the human body all the way to a tree. How can people not love science?"

Instead of (1) teaching rules, (2) drilling the rules, (3) practicing using the rules, and (4) testing knowledge of the rules, let's begin with patterns. When students are struggling to learn it is almost always because what they are studying doesn't make sense. Patterns make sense to everyone. When approaching a new topic, regardless of the age of the students, teachers would save a great deal of time and students' intrinsic motivation if the unit began with patterns. It will seem like starting with patterns will take more time. It may take more time initially, but because students actually understand what is being taught significant time is saved in the future.

CHAPTER 24

Remember When___? I did it!

The outcomes are improvement projects that are coming out of this (deep learning) in terms of the creativity, their impact that they can have on society on local or larger problems.

Michael Fullan

Remember when_____? I did it!

The assignment from the university junior in teacher preparation was to write a 32-page picture book. The pattern is:

Page 1   Remember when ...
Page 2   (Description of a family crisis)
Page 3   and nobody would admit who did it?
Page 4   I did not do it.
Page 5   Remember when ...
Page 6   (Another family crisis)
Page 7   and nobody would admit who did it?
Page 8   I did not do it.
(Pages 9–28 followed the same pattern with a new family crisis
    described each time.)
Page 29   Remember when ...
Page 30   (Description of the final family crisis)
Page 31   and nobody would admit who did it?
Page 32   I did it.

The 32-page picture-book assignment is an example of the type of assignments that cannot be evaluated by simple counting. Scales of quality must be created. In education these are labeled rubrics. If readers look on the internet for "education rubrics examples," there are hundreds of examples available by clicking on "view all images." Be sure not to hit the print command unless you have an ample supply of printer ink and copy paper available. You will see that all of the rubric examples are structured as a matrix. In this chapter you will learn about a better structure—the dichotomous rubric that asks yes/no questions.

There are three reasons the dichotomous rubric is an improvement over the matrix rubric: (1) students have a much more clear idea of the teacher's expectations, (2) continuous improvement can be graphed because the results are more accurate and consistent, and (3) students are usually 90% accurate in self-assessing their rubric score prior to the teacher's assessment. Ever since Nicole Trovillian created the five-point dichotomous rubrics for six-traits writing (posted at www.LBellJ.com), I have been enamored with her structure, graphics, precision, and the five-point design of a dichotomous rubric. The reason is that the fifth point can provide the opportunity to give credit for more than requested, required, or expected. The patterned book referenced above was far better than expected. It could be duplicated for many family members and friends. If I had known of the dichotomous rubric at that time, I would have written the final rubric question as, "Is this draft manuscript publishable?"

Susan Barnes, a California high-school music teacher, created a dichotomous rubric (Figure 24.1) to evaluate small-group vocal performances. She wrote, "My students especially like the opportunity to earn five points as opposed to four for going above and beyond. The fifth point really gives them license to be creative and innovative in their performances."

In order to preserve and further polish intrinsic motivation it is very important to give students accurate feedback on their project-based assignments. That is why the rubrics in this chapter were created by teachers. You will see that they make sense to the students, and that is why the self-assessment is so accurate. The yes/no questions have far less value judgment, which is valuable for both students and teachers.

Fig. 24.1

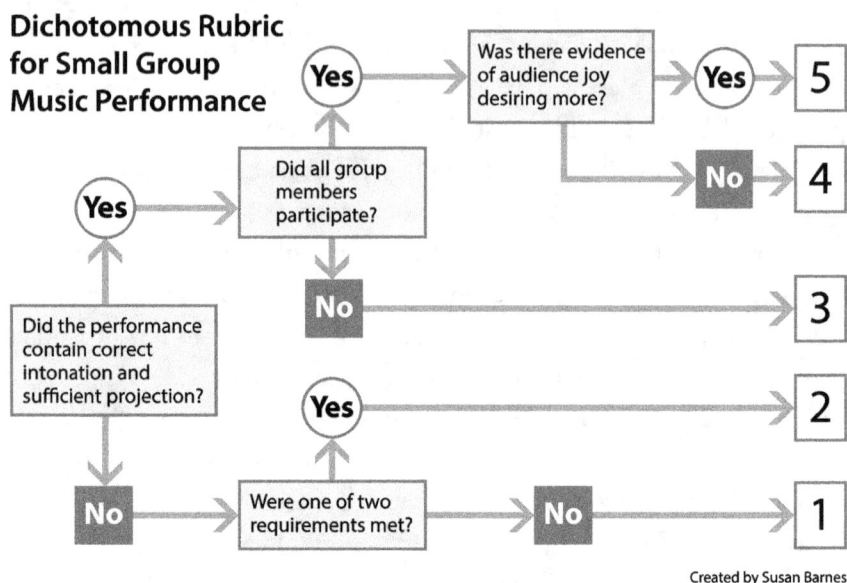

Dichotomous Rubric for Small Group Music Performance

Created by Susan Barnes

The layout is clear, without hidden expectations or room for teachers to grade based on their opinions or abstract requirements.

When teachers implement the LtoJ process described in Part III, they save considerable amounts of surface-learning instructional time. Saving time coupled with increased learning is a the outcome from using these rubrics. This saved time is used for deep and transfer-learning. The contents of this chapter will continue the same pattern with deep learning—better results in less time.

In my experience creating courses, I have found the dichotomous rubric to be clear and helpful to students. For example, in the AdvancED course, Basic Data for Continuous Improvement, dichotomous rubrics are provided for each of the projects. Figure 24.2 is a dichotomous rubric for the assignment to create a radar chart. As shown below, students are able to easily assess whether or not they are meeting the standards placed on them for the project by following the arrows for each expectation. Clear grading expectations saves time for both students and teachers.

Dichotomous rubrics are useful for other arenas outside of grading

Fig. 24.2

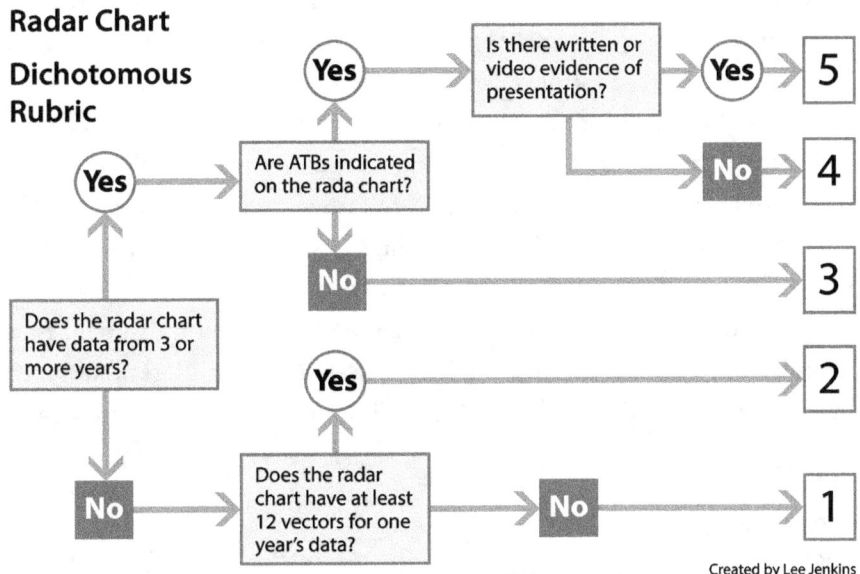

Radar Chart

Dichotomous Rubric

Created by Lee Jenkins

classroom projects. In the personnel chapter of *Optimize Your School*, I used Nicole's format for the dichotomous rubric to enhance conversations between the principals and teachers. The last question on this rubric asks, "Is the teacher of significant help to colleagues?" Teachers are not hired to help other teachers; they are hired to assist students. School systems do not expect this level of leadership, but can honor it when it occurs. For this reason I like the five-point rubric; it gives a way to honor work that is far beyond what is expected.

The remainder of this chapter offers dichotomous rubrics written by various K–12 educators for projects they assign in their classrooms. These are not easy to write, but are much easier to implement than matrix rubrics.

Bill Watkins, superintendent of Oregon's Marcola School District, spent numerous years as a wrestling coach. Each match is a one-on-one competition, and he had to figure out a way to help his athletes develop perseverance when they continually lost matches and were tempted to give up. His solution was to develop a rubric in order to give continuous improvement scores after each match. He writes, "Telling wrestlers (who continue to lose matches) they are improving was not enough to keep them motivated to continue wrestling. I needed some data they could embrace to show their improvement and motivate them to continue putting in the extra effort it takes to ultimately improve their individual win/loss record." In using the rubric Watkins created, students walked off the mat with their head high and wanted to know their rubric score. There were celebrations of individual All-Time Bests, as well as team ATBs when all of the individual scores were added together. Bill's team later placed second in the Alaska state tournament—an accomplishment that would never have occurred if his formerly struggling athletes had given up too soon. Figure 24.3 shows Bill's dichotomous rubric for wrestling.

Fig. 24.3

Wrestling Dichotomous Rubric

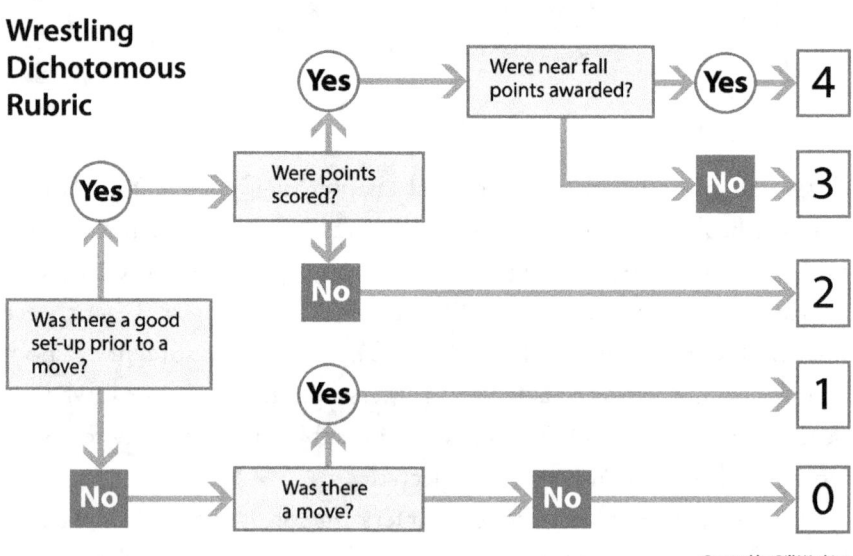

Created by Bill Watkins

Julie Sprague and Allen Culp, Grade 7 teachers in language arts and social studies, respectively, combine efforts each year to teach an interdisciplinary unit. They use two dichotomous rubrics to first give students a very clear picture of expectations and secondly to use for final evaluation of the work. The thinking that went into creating the rubrics is the hard part—lots of wordsmithing, but readers will learn from their final rubric. Enjoy Figures 24.4 and 24.5.

Fig. 24.4

Change

Dichotomous Rubric:
What is change?
What affects change?

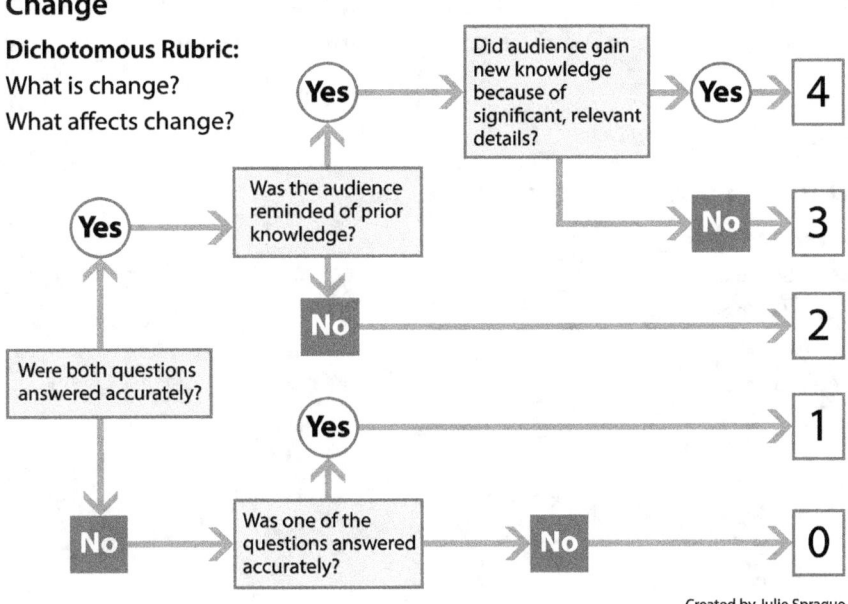

Created by Julie Sprague

Fig. 24.5

Change

Dichotomous Rubric:
What is change?
What affects change?

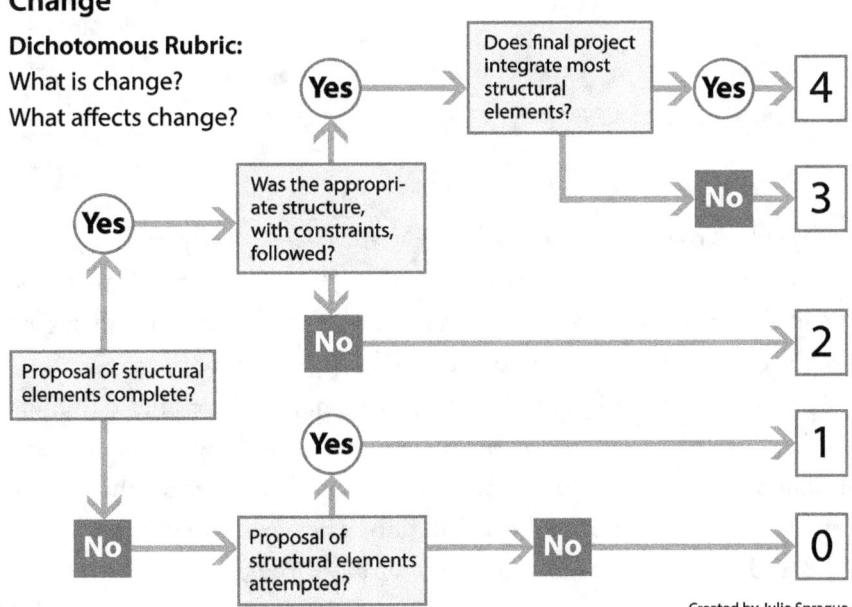

Created by Julie Sprague

Just across the hallway is the science classroom taught by Sujata Kumar. Below is her dichotomous rubric (Figure 24.6) for a STEM project with the same Grade 7 students using the prior two dichotomous rubrics.

Fig. 24.6

Dichotomous Rubric for Engineering

Invention Project for one of 4 areas:

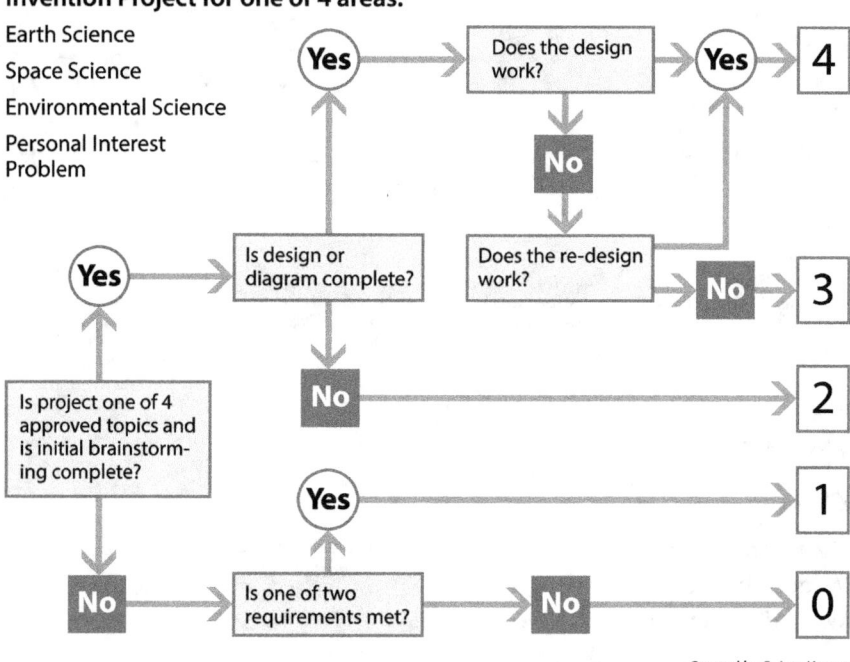

Earth Science

Space Science

Environmental Science

Personal Interest Problem

Created by Sujata Kumar

Nicole Trovillion created the math-problem-solving rubric below. (Figure 24.7) It is written to solve the ongoing problem of giving no credit for an incorrect answer with a successful process or for giving no credit for a correct answer with a limited explanation of the process.

Chassie Capps of Lake Havasu, Arizona, has her middle-school students write and then present their research on how mathematics is used in various occupations. She created two rubrics: one for the written report and one for the oral presentation. They are below. (See Figures 24.8 and 24.9). It is often true that not all of the expectations for one

Fig. 24.7

Dichotomous Rubric for Mathematics
Open Ended Response (OER)

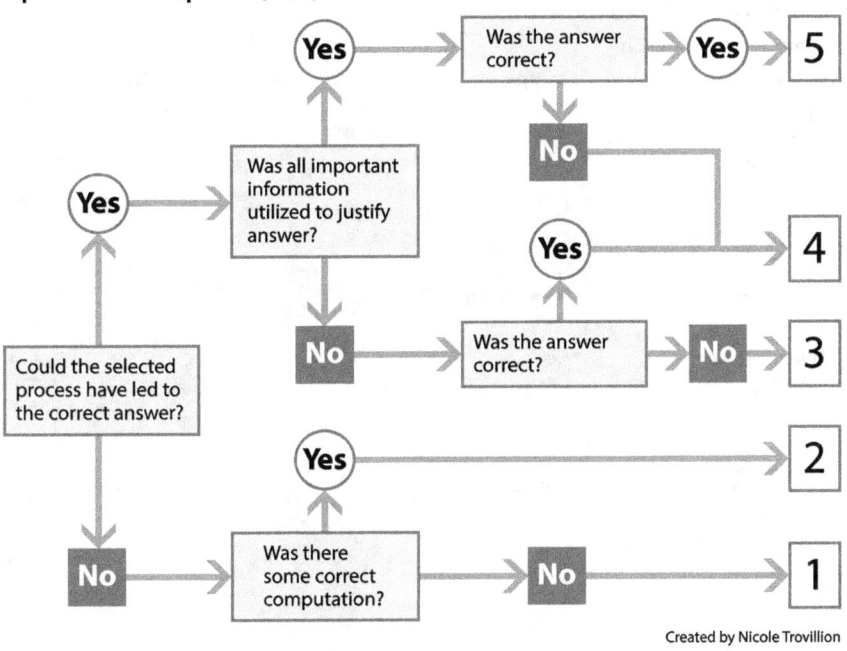

Created by Nicole Trovillion

aspect of education can be placed on one dichotomous rubric. Dividing up the oral from the written requirements allows the rubric to still make sense to students and not overwhelm them with too many aspects in any one rubric.

The rubric written by Shannaca Karlin for the Nebraska map (Figure 24.10) has a couple of variations. The scale is 0–4 instead of 1–5, as is also true for some of the earlier rubrics in Chapter 24. This clearly is up to the teachers creating the rubric and the school structure where they teach. Further, there is the use of the asterisk to indicate that more details are printed on the back of the rubric. This includes a list of the geographic locations that must be on the map. Also note that not every rubric with a 1–5 scale uses the 5 to indicate a result of "above expectations." Designers have both content and structural decisions to make with dichotomous rubrics.

Fig. 24.8

Dichotomous Rubric for Mathematics Career: Written Report

Write: Results from 3 interviews re: careers using math
Present: Speech about 3 chosen careers
Visuals: Used in speech
Time: 4–6 minutes
Purpose: Learn how mathematics is used in multiple careers

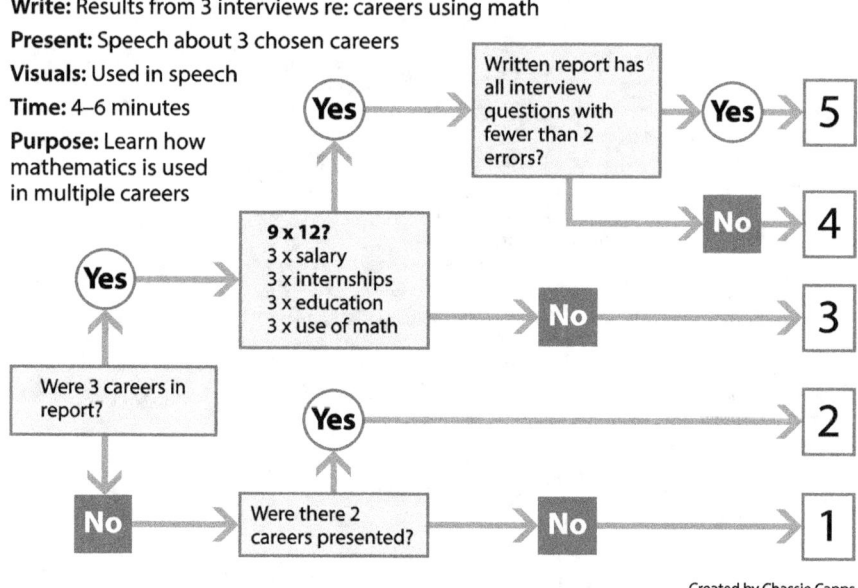

9 x 12?
3 x salary
3 x internships
3 x education
3 x use of math

Written report has all interview questions with fewer than 2 errors? → Yes → 5 / No → 4

No → 3

Were 3 careers in report?

Yes → 2

No → Were there 2 careers presented? → No → 1

Fig. 24.9

Dichotomous Rubric for Mathematics Career: Oral Presentation

Write: Results from 3 interviews re: careers using math
Present: Speech about 3 chosen careers
Visuals: Used in speech
Time: 4–6 minutes
Purpose: Learn how mathematics is used in multiple careers

Yes → Could people in back of room hear presentation? → Yes → 5 / No → 4

Yes → Did the presentation take between 4 and 6 minutes? → No → 3

Was more than one visual used in the presentation?

Yes → 2

No → Was one visual used in the presentation? → No → 1

Fig. 24.10

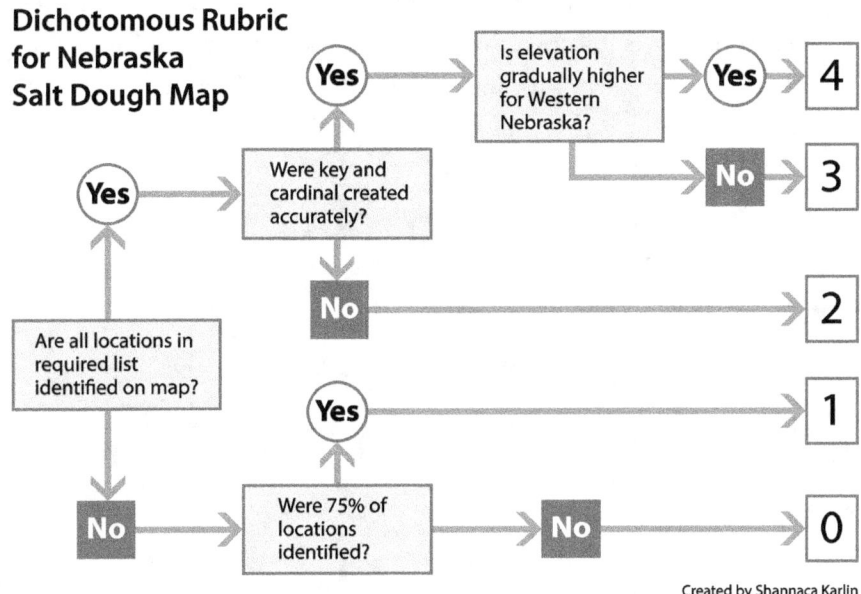

Dichotomous Rubric for Nebraska Salt Dough Map

Created by Shannaca Karlin

On LBellJ.com, under free resources/dichotomous rubrics, there are not only example rubrics, but also a blank PowerPoint rubric ready for people to enter their criteria. Also on the website are blank graphs for dichotomous rubrics. These are designed for educators who are continually assessing students on deep-learning assignments and want to document improvement over the course of a school year.

In Chapter 13, I outlined the process for educators to provide lists of surface-learning for the entire year. I never discount the knowledge and time it takes to construct such a list. It is time consuming to remove the trivia from the list and then to coordinate with other grade levels to eliminate duplicates. I actually do not know which is harder—creating the key-concept lists for surface-learning or creating dichotomous rubrics for deep learning. What I do know is that neither is easy *and* that both are so very powerful in (1) communicating to students the expectations and (2) evaluating the student work in such a way that students and teachers arrive at the same score. I placed this chapter under the heading "Polish Perfect" because deep-learning assignments can create such student joy and feelings of accomplishment. However, if students feel the expectations for deep-learning are confusing or the evaluation is loaded with far too many subjective/favoritism components, the polish is soon removed from deep-learning and the all-important intrinsic motivation is damaged.

CHAPTER 25

Parents Are Amazed at What They Learn from a Ten-Year Old

Hope is a gift. Have you ever taken hold of such a prize that leads you out of uncertainty into profound assurance? If so, you have possessed hope.

Billy Graham

Mrs. Anderson, principal, welcomes the kindergarten parents again for the monthly meeting. She reminds the parents that they are scheduled to visit a Grade 5 classroom taught by Mrs. Codi Hrouda today. Anderson stated, "She has been working with Lee Jenkins for over a dozen years. You will see the principles and practices that have been briefly explained in our meetings. You are welcome to stay all morning in her room. I do need one parent to jot down times and activities and another parent to write down what you learn from the students when they are completing their graphing responsibilities. You will share your observations at our next meeting. You are expected to arrive in Mrs. Hrouda's classroom at nine this morning. A guest teacher will be in her room for five minutes because our school is celebrating a school-wide All-Time Best in math fluency last week. To celebrate, the teachers are switching classrooms in order to share a favorite story, poem, book, or song for five minutes. Mrs. Hrouda will return to her room to greet all of her visitors at 9:06."

The parents arrived in Mrs. Hrouda's room at 9:00. One month later . . .

At the next monthly meeting, the two parents assigned to take notes shared their observations from the prior month's visit. The first parent recorded the schedule and the second parent collected the overall observations during the graphing time.

9:06 Mrs. Hrouda returns to her classroom, welcomes kindergarten parents and prepares for math quiz.

9:07 Students are given a non-graded math quiz—number 14 of 28 for the year.

Questions are randomly selected from end-of-year standards.

9:27 Time for quiz is over. Codi collects quizzes for her to score. Students are placed in groups of 3–4. Each group is given a new copy of the quiz and told to reach agreement on correct answers for every question. Each group must also agree on answers with one other group in the classroom. Codi scores individual student quizzes while this activity is taking place.

9:35 Codi returns scored, individual, non-graded quizzes and checks to be sure each group completed their agreements on the correct answers for each problem.

9:36 Each student places a dot on the data collector indicating their number of correct answers. No names are on the collector. Each student also completes an individual graph for their number correct.

9:40 Codi goes over quiz, spending more time on questions about topics already taught than questions about things that will be taught later.

9:50 Students have assigned responsibilities after each of the LtoJ quizzes. They jump up immediately to complete their jobs. Students are assigned to one of the following responsibilities:

Scatter Diagram
Class Run Chart
Histogram

Item Analysis
Effect Size Calculator
All-Time Best Distribution Center
Calculation of Mean, Median, Mode, and Range
Average score from most recent Will & Thrill Matrix

9:50 Students currently without an assigned responsibility have an early start on their math assignment. Six students are asked to bring up their personal math book. Two are assigned square roots with fractions, two receive a counting assignment with mixed numerals, and two are asked to calculate the percentage of classroom wall space covered by paper. (They are informed the fire marshal is coming soon). Remaining students know the fraction center where they are assigned for the week and start early on some difficult if/then fraction logic questions.

9:53 The two students assigned to the class run chart announce that the class had their fifth All-Time Best in math. Codi states they will celebrate just before library check out at 10:35.

9:53 As students complete their responsibilities for the graphing of the most recent math LtoJ quiz, they gradually move onto their assigned fraction center for the week. The five centers all use different materials.

10:30 Codi asks students to clean up the fraction materials and be ready in two minutes for the ATB celebration.

10:32 Codi and students celebrate by singing Father Abraham. Because it was their fifth ATB, they sang up to the fifth motion.

10:35 Library Check Out

10:50 Return from Library Check Out

10:51 Codi shares a two-week trial of two ideas gleaned from the Will & Thrill Feedback form filled out by students. She explains the ideas that will be used in language arts. In two weeks, students are told they can vote whether or not to keep the ideas. One idea was given to help students exert more effort (Will) and one is given to help students enjoy the learning more (Thrill).

10:54 Codi gives the new language arts assignment. Students are to prove they understand these three literary terms. They are told three ways they can prove their knowledge, but are also informed that if they have another idea, to come see her.

After this time-based sequence was shared by the first parent, a second parent reported to the rest of the parent group, stating, "There were six of us who were able to remain with Mrs. Hrouda's classroom until eleven in the morning. We now understand how the enthusiasm our children have for school in kindergarten can be maintained all the way through high school.

> ... we want to have more ATBs, which is actually quite hard.

"We hope all of you can make arrangements to visit Mrs. Hrouda's classroom. It is amazing how much we learned from 10-year-old students regarding how to keep track of learning progress. These students are more capable than 95% of adults in this arena. Before we go into detail, it is important to share the most consistent observation. The students see themselves as a learning team helping each other. Every student takes joy in both their personal improvement and team improvement.

"Mrs. Hrouda's class takes six of the LtoJ quizzes almost each week—seven times a quarter, to be exact. If you go to the classroom, the first graph the students show you is the scatter diagram. It is simply a dot for the number of questions correct for each student, every quiz. There are no names, just dots. When we were in the room, some of us asked, 'Why do your dots go down some of the time?' The answer was, 'Sometimes the questions are harder, more challenging questions than on previous quizzes.'

'Do students work hard to move the dots higher?'

'Yes, actually because we want to have more ATBs, which is actually quite hard.' 'When other students have an ATB, what happens?'

'We high five them, or say, "Good job, keep up the hard work!"'

'We heard some students talking and they said the scatter diagram was their favorite graph. We then asked students why this was true.

'They said, 'Because everyone can find their own dots and know that their score helped add to the class total each week.'

'This caused us to ask about bullying. We asked, 'Have you ever heard of students picking on another because of a low score?'

'Never. We all are a team, and each person matters in our team effort. We know that some members of our team are going to have a bad day, just like some of our teammates have bad games in sports, but we know that they will work hard to bring up their score because they want the team to succeed.'

"The students then pointed out to us that they use the dots on the scatter diagram to count up the total for the class to see if they earned an ATB.

"Next the students showed us their class run chart. We asked, 'What is this chart telling us?'

'Actually,' they said, 'There are two run charts—one for each student and one for the whole class. This one tells us how we are doing as a class and how many ATBs we've had.'

'How is your class run chart doing currently?' 'It goes up most weeks.'

'What about at the beginning of the year? I see that in the whole class there were only 16 correct questions on affixes.'

'We knew that we would get better. This week our class had 66 correct answers out of 140 possible and it is only February.'

'What is the hardest quiz?' 'Affixes.'

'What is the easiest quiz?' 'Vocabulary.'

'So,' we asked, 'How do you obtain the number of correct answers for the whole class?'

'We count up the dots on the scatter diagram. So, if three of us have eight correct answers, then we write down 24, then if six of us have seven correct, we write down 42 and so on. We add up all of these numbers for the class run chart.'

"The third quiz the students taught us about is called the histogram. We adults knew the most famous histogram, the bell curve, but we learned a lot. The students taught us that in the beginning of the year, there is an *L* curve and then a bell curve most of the year. They said they were working hard to get to a *J* curve by the end of the year.

"We asked, 'Do your parents know what a histogram is?' 'No.'

"Then we observed that some of the histograms were not plain graphs, but had art. The students said, 'Well, it is easy to see that this histogram was made to show Christmas presents. This histogram shows the towers of 9-11.'

Fig. 25.1

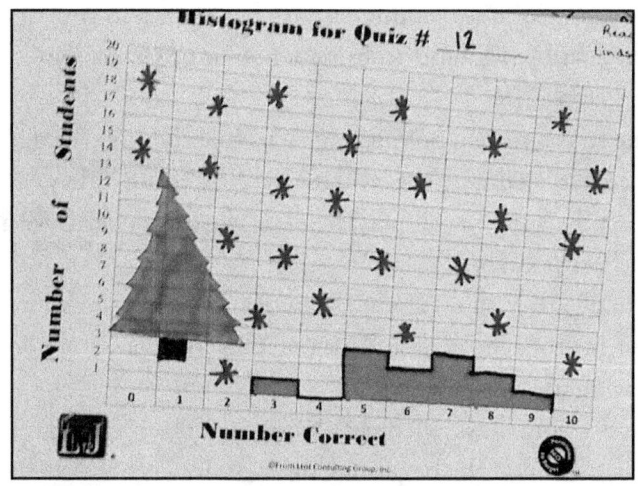

Fig. 25.2

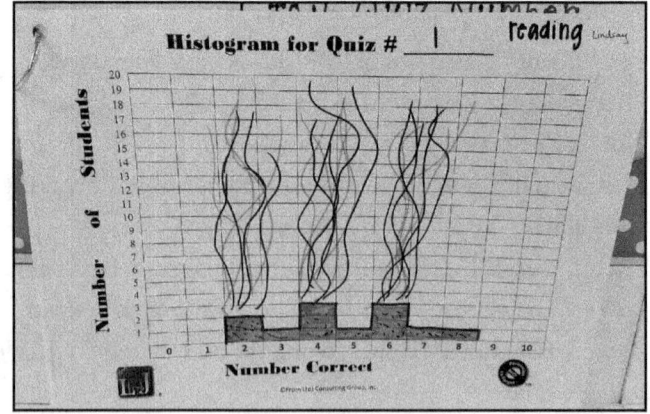

"It was amazing for the six of us to see that from the dots on the scatter diagram, students created the class run chart and the histograms.

"We moved onto the fourth graph—Item Analysis.

"We heard, 'This graph shows what we missed the most all the way to questions nobody missed. It is for the whole class.'

'Is it helpful?'

'Yes, it tells us what we need to work on, so we can practice and never miss those questions again.'

'Are you disappointed sometimes?'

'Only when a lot of us miss a third- or fourth-grade question, or a fifth-grade question that we should all know because it has been taught and practiced many times throughout the year.'

'What happens then?'

We say to each other, 'Come on guys; we can do better than that!'

"The next stop on our tour was with the students calculating mean, median, mode, and range. We asked if they could tell us the results from a recent quiz. They said that on the math standards quiz they had a median of six, a mean of 5 and 6 tenths, two modes of four and seven, and a range of eight. This is for a 10-item quiz.

"We thought that this might be a hard job, but they replied, 'Not really. Yes, it was hard in the beginning of the year, but easy now.'

'How long does this take you?' 'Five minutes.'

'Could you have a mode of 10 by the end of the year?' 'Definitely.'

"Next, we moved onto the Will & Thrill Matrix. We also had not heard of this either, but we learned quickly.

'What is happening here?'

'Mrs. Hrouda wants us to work very hard and to love working hard at school. So, when it is time for another Will & Thrill matrix, she gives each of us a mini-matrix. We each put an x on our mini and then a couple kids place all of the x's onto the larger matrix. This gives us a picture of how hard we are working and how much we like the class. Then we use this sheet to score all of the x's and average the score.'

"We noticed that there were a lot of x's near the upper right corner. They said, "Yes, there are three x's with 100% effort and loving school learning, but then there are others who are 75% effort/Love or 100% effort/Like.' They said their average on the Will & Thrill Matrix was seven and eight tenths with nine being perfect.

"The two students then showed us the feedback form. It was used for students to give Mrs. Hrouda the students' perspective on what would help them work harder and what would help them enjoy school more. One suggestion to help them work harder was to implement extra computer time for any students who had personal ATBs or for the entire class when they had a class ATB. A suggestion to help them enjoy school more was for her to incorporate more student-created technology that shows their learning and/or set their learning time to music.

"Our last stop was a completely new item called the LtoJ Effect-Size Calculator. We had never heard of this before, but once students explained it to us, we understood how important this tool is to classroom assessment.

"They said, 'We enter the numbers from the scatter diagram dots into the computer at the end of each quarter. It tells us how our class is doing compared to the average learning in a classroom. We learned that the average effect size from a normal classroom is .40. So, each quarter we observe how we are doing compared to this worldwide learning average. It makes us feel great and causes us to work harder. For example, at the end of first semester we had a .92 on affixes.'

"Think about it: more than double a year's learning in half a year. These students also ran the ATB Distribution Center. They showed us how individual students who prove they had an ATB on a quiz receive a sticker to place above the column on their student run chart with the new ATB. This allows them to easily count up the number of ATBs for the whole year. Then they give out a cut-out of a cardinal to write their name and the subject in which they achieved the ATB.

"We asked several groups of the students what their favorite way was to celebrate classroom ATBs. They all agreed that rolling a die to see how they were going to celebrate was their favorite. Before we left, we asked Mrs. Hrouda to tell us her perspective from a teacher's point of view. She said, "Before implementing LtoJ with my classes, I was doing all of the work when it came to tracking student data and trying to motivate students to achieve academic success. My students were clueless as to what standards they were to master for the entire year, and I felt they were not invested in their learning. I also felt there was a divide amongst the students in my room who were earning good grades and those who were not. Neither side understood the other and did little to encourage one another or work together to help each other achieve success. After implementing LtoJ, my classes are now self-tracking, self-motivated, and community oriented. They encourage each other to do well and even volunteer to help each other practice or study a concept that one of their peers needs help reviewing. All of my students can tell you exactly what they know and what they still need to learn or master. This process of LtoJ has changed me too. The students' learning drives my instruction now. I listen to their suggestions on how to help them work harder and to make learning fun. They know that their voices are heard, and I value all of their input and efforts throughout their learning journey. I used to believe that I got into teaching because I loved watching the light come on for kids when they learned something new, but now with LtoJ, it is more than that. I not only love watching the light come on for my students, but also their priceless expressions when they realize they can remember these concepts even if they learned them at the beginning of the year and we are now in the third quarter. My heart soars with theirs when I watch them track their learning and they realize they have a personal ATB, even if it is just by one point, and I cheer as loud as they do when the class gets an ATB. LtoJ has brought out the kindergartner in me as a teacher, in the sense that I get so excited about my students' learning and I look forward to each day at school with them to help them continue achieving success not only academically, but socially and emotionally as well.'"

> **LtoJ has brought out the kindergartner in me as a teacher**

Mrs. Anderson then stated that this past week Mrs. Hrouda's classroom had All-Time Bests on five of their six LtoJ quizzes. She had never had this happen before. She read a quotation from John Hattie: "'What works best for students is similar to what works best for teachers (Hattie, 2009, p.IV).' Dr. Hattie could probably change his statement to: 'What works best for students is similar to what works best for both teachers and parents.' The gift of hope is what you observed and what we wish for all of our students regardless of their prior disappointments."

She closed by stating that the teachers have asked parents to design a report card from parents to teachers. "At our next meeting we will start the design of this feedback to the teachers. I will not be reading these report cards from you; they are for our teachers' eyes only. It will be helpful for everyone.

"Thank you for joining me today and for the parents who were able to observe Mrs. Hrouda's classroom. We are so excited to have parents learning about the processes with LtoJ that maintain the intrinsic motivation so prevalent in kindergarten. Helping our students, parents, and teachers as they become more and more excited about learning is not only my goal, but my passion. I am thankful that you have had the chance to take part in such an innovative form of education. I am excited to see what expectations and feedback you will have for our teachers and for me. Have a great month."

CHAPTER 26

Research

Fundamentally, the most powerful way of thinking about a teacher's role is for teachers to see themselves as evaluators of their effects on students. Teachers need to use evidence-based methods to inform, change and sustain these evaluation beliefs about their effect.

John Hattie, 2012

John Hattie's work is significant in the pursuit of *How to Create a Perfect School*. His knowledge was instrumental in several capacities: (1) how to research the impact of the LtoJ approach with the LtoJ Effect-Size Calculator, (2) the *Visible Learning* research that explains why the LtoJ process works so well, (3) the triplets of Skill, Will, and Thrill that are the foundation for measuring intrinsic motivation, (4) the persuasive research detailing how surface-learning and automaticity are essential for success with deep-learning, the (5) one-on-one conversations, and (6) the ongoing mentoring through emails between Scottsdale, Arizona, USA, and Melbourne, Victoria, Australia.

This is not a research article like you would read in a scientific journal; it is a story of inspiration that led to years of research and eventually this book. For years, I had been told that research on the LtoJ process was necessary. I did not disagree. The problem was the medical model for research; I was supposed to randomly select control classrooms that were not using LtoJ to compare to classrooms using LtoJ. For many practical reasons, including parent permissions for their children to participate in an experiment, this was not practical.

At Corwin's annual Visible Learning Conference in 1996, Doug Fisher stated in his keynote that everyone could calculate effect sizes. A light bulb went off in my brain; this statement clearly got my attention. Fisher's opening encouragement was followed by the events with Hattie described in Chapter 22.

After the conference I searched on the internet for the formula for effect size and also read more details. Effect sizes can be used to compare an experimental group with a control group. They can also be used for pre- and post-test assessments. It was pre- and post-test data that matched with my and John Hattie's mantra that teachers should know their impact. So, once I had the formula, I wrote to teachers I had worked with in various places and had them simply photograph their scatter diagrams from the prior year(s) and send them to me. The effect size for 61 classrooms was calculated to be an average of 3.01. Obviously, with the average influence from Hattie's Visible Learning at 0.40, I was quite thrilled.

I suspected that this effect size was higher than could be expected because the 61 classrooms represented teachers with between three and fifteen years' experience with the LtoJ process. I averaged all of the effect sizes for the next two years. There are now 311 classrooms with an average effect size of 2.34. The total number of students in the research is 7,775 and the number of quizzes is approximately 217,700. It does look like this average influence is going to hold very steady. 2.34 divided by the average influence upon student learning (0.40) is 5.85. No influence upon student learning, to my knowledge, has had this high an effect size. Why?

I believe the answer is that the LtoJ process combines a dozen or more of the most impactful influences upon student learning into one process. The *Visible Learning* research of over 250 influences are all studies of single influences, one at a time. It is common sense that if a process combines a dozen of these influences, that the effect size will be higher than any one individual influence. Readers should bookmark www.VisibleLearningPlus.com and then click on the research tab in order to understand what works best in education and what is popular but is not working. One example of something that is not working well is trying to understand and teach to different learning styles. "There is not any recognized evidence suggesting that knowing or diagnosing learning styles will help you to teach your students any better than not knowing their learning style" (Hattie and Yates, 2014, p. 176). "Ninety-five percent of changes made by management today make no improvement" (Deming, 1994, p. 38). This observation by Deming alone is reason enough to check out the Hattie research.

The other reason for the high effect size is the ability of various schools to replicate the process. "The capacity to replicate quality outcomes on a regular basis becomes the ultimate gold standard" (Byrk et al., 2015, p. 186).

In the 1950s it took eight days for longshoremen to empty a ship's cargo and eight days for longshoremen to load the ship back up, one article at a time. The ship could be loaded with up to 194,582 separate items. Malcolm McLean had a better idea; he invented the cargo ship. "It was forty times more productive than a longshoremen's crew with their winches, pallets, and hooks" (Baker, 2016, p. 34). When I observe what is happening in schools with new federal and state laws, court decisions, state initiatives, board policies, and ever-changing superintendents/priorities, I think education needs something like container ships. If readers think that 194,582 items on a ship has nothing to do with education, one visit to an education attorney's office and the sight of all the legal, education-specific books therein will dispel this thought.

The combining of powerful influences from Hattie's *Visible Learning* research into the single LtoJ process is similar to a container on a ship. What other of education's 194,582 initiatives can be combined to increase engagement, efficiency, and effectiveness?

The influences and their effect sizes that are imbedded into the LtoJ process are below:

Self-reported grades (sometimes reported as Assessment   1.33
    Capable Students)
Formative Assessment   .72

Acceleration	.68
Classroom Management	.75
Teacher Clarity	.75
Feedback	.74
Teacher-Student Relationships	.52
Massed versus Spaced Out Assessment	.58
Collective Teacher Efficacy	1.39
Teacher Credibility	1.09
Setting Standards for Self-Judgment	.75
Prior Ability	.98

Each of the dozen influences upon student learning are inserted into the normal classroom operation, as in a ship container, with the LtoJ process and a *How to Create a Perfect School* mindset. Comments on each of the 12 follow:

1. Creating assessment-capable students (1.33) is a major focus LtoJ. Instead of having assessment-capable software programmers, we need assessment-capable students. Providing software for the teacher to use after school defeats the purpose of student engagement with the data. Almost all school systems now provide computerized grading software for teachers to use. It has no influence upon student learning whatsoever. It may save the teacher time or it may take the teacher more time, but the software doesn't increase learning. Likewise, having software create all of the LtoJ graphs will do nothing for creating assessment-capable students. The statement by Codi Hrouda at the end of Chapter 25 is one of the most powerful examples of assessment-capable students you will ever read.

2. Formative assessment (0.72) with LtoJ is a non-graded quiz on a randomly selected set of key concepts drawn from a whole year's key concepts. Like other formative assessments

it is non-graded, but unlike most formative assessments it is always assessing the whole year's content, plus, very often, prior year's content.

3. Acceleration (0.68) with LtoJ occurs when a student has seven perfect quizzes in a row. It is at that time that the student has proven with 99% assurance they know the surface-learning for the whole year and have earned the privilege to start early on the next year's surface-learning. These students will still need to utilize this knowledge with grade level deep-learning assignments. I am pleased with the criteria for acceleration because "it is perhaps tempting in a competitive society where productivity is emphasized, to think in terms of speeding up the child's progress through the levels of development in order to induce the earlier acquisition of abstract concepts" (Neufeld, 1972, p. 40). With the criteria of seven perfect quizzes in a row, students earn the right to be accelerated and they know they achieved it without their parents pressuring the teacher.

The statistical proof that the student can be accelerated is the flip of a coin probability. If a student answers all questions correctly on an LtoJ quiz, there is a 50% chance the student is lucky.

All questions correct on two quizzes in a row = 25% chance lucky. All questions correct on three quizzes in a row = 12.5% chance lucky. All questions correct on four quizzes in a row = 6.25% chance lucky. All questions correct on five quizzes in a row = 3.12% chance lucky. All questions correct on six quizzes in a row = 1.56% chance lucky. All questions correct on seven quizzes in a row = .75% chance lucky.

The standard for acceleration is very high, but is achieved by a few students in almost every classroom that is utilizing LtoJ. Combined with this research of the positives of acceleration is that "there were negative effects if not accelerated" (Hattie, 2009, p. 101).

4. Classroom management (0.75) is a very strange influence to include with a feedback system. The basic reason why LtoJ improves classroom behavior is that the students become much more intrinsically motivated to do well. They want to improve personally and also want to contribute to classroom improvement. Teachers are not wasting time trying to redirect students to tasks, and students are less inclined to act out because they are bored.

5 Teacher clarity (0.75) begins the first day of school, when the students receive the list of key concepts for the year. It is further reinforced all year when the teachers inform the students which key concept is being taught during a particular day or week. Then, with deep-learning assignments students are provided dichotomous rubrics—even more clarity! Of course, the instruction has to make sense to the students. This is the major aspect of teacher clarity, but clarity for the year sets the stage for continual success.

6. Feedback (0.74) goes in two directions: teacher to student and student to teacher. The LtoJ process described in Part III is almost exclusively feedback from student to their teacher. The students are telling the teacher what learning is in their long-term memory as they proceed from the beginning of a school year on to the end of the year. Everyone knows if the class is on target to meet end-of-the-year standards. (i.e. if the class has used 60% of the year's time, do the students know 60% of the content?)

7. Teacher-Student Relationships (0.52) are strengthened through all of the aspects of *How to Create a Perfect School*: The Will & Thrill process, not demoralizing students in the ways described in Part II, using data for joyful evidence of learning, and then the polishing of perfect. I remember the first time a teacher told me how much the LtoJ process helped

his relationship with his students. Actually, I was surprised and wanted to know more about how this could happen. He said it was because of the class run chart. The students and the teacher all wanted the class run chart to increase and thus it put everyone on the same team instead of being adversaries arguing over a grade. With the Will & Thrill Feedback form, students have evidence that the teacher is listening to them and implementing their ideas.

8. Massed versus Spaced Out Assessment (0.58) creates 1.5 times the average learning by simply spacing out the assessments. We know that almost all assessments in the United States are massed with chapter and unit tests. Even quarterly assessments are for the current quarter only. The LtoJ process spaces out the assessment over the whole year or beyond. Ideally, all assessments would include preview of yet-to-be- taught content, plus review of prior current year content. Spacing out the assessments does a great deal to remove the pervasive permission to forget practices. "The difficulty of spaced repetition is not effort but that it requires forward planning and a small investment of time to set up a system. But in the long run, it saves us time as we retain information and spend less total time learning" (Farnam Street).

9. Collective teacher efficacy (1.39) is so powerful and yet so difficult to attain in most schools. When the totals of every classroom are added up for grade level, department, and school, everyone can see what they are accomplishing together. These graphs, posted in hallways, are a major step toward having collective teacher efficacy. The graphs create the feeling of "look what we have accomplished thus far and we have____ % of the year left." Further, collective efficacy is maximized when the effect sizes for all classrooms are averaged quarterly. The whole school knows how they are doing TOGETHER. When teachers learn, for example, that at the end of the first

quarter the effect size for their school is approximately 0.40, they are ready to tackle even more learning. A team of teachers knowing that their students have learned in a quarter what most schools learn in a full year is collective teacher efficacy dosed with energy.

10. Teacher credibility (1.09) is far more than an engaging personality; it is student confidence that the teacher knows and has organized the content and cares deeply that the students learn the content. Knowledge without caring or caring without knowledge does not equal credibility. The strategies outlined in Part I are about caring; students know the teachers desire that they maintain their intrinsic motivation and are willing to listen to student ideas. Part II illustrates strategies that communicate care by eliminating the practices that demoralize so many students. Parts III and IV contribute to credibility through organization of the content.

11. Setting standards for self-judgment (0.75) is a key aspect of *How to Create a Perfect School*. It comes through continual evidence that I am improving my knowledge of surface-learning with quizzes and my ability to solve deep-learning problems utilizing the dichotomous rubrics. The assessments of many project-based student works are often confusing, which cause students to believe a poor assessment means the teacher does not like them. Teachers have found that with the dichotomous rubric students are approximately 90% accurate in predicting the teacher's rubric score.

12. Prior ability (0.98) correlates highly to success during the current year. I think readers already know this to be true. Students with good grades last year will most likely have good grades this year. We can increase the percentage of students who earn good grades because they actually remember the content and deserve the good grades. When teachers use the dichotomous

rubric, for example, with all of their project-based assignments, more students will score higher because the expectations are so clear. Higher rubric scores equal better grades, which is a prior ability correlating positively with success the next year.

Research is often so overwhelming. Hattie has made it accessible to all of us in an accessible format. That is what he has done for me; I now have the research to understand why the LtoJ process and the concepts in *How to Create a Perfect School* are so effective. Further, teachers train students to enter the data from their classroom scatter diagram into the LtoJ Effect-Size Calculator and know the effect size for their classroom. Principals can average the effect sizes of all classrooms and have the effect size for their school. Now that makes research meaningful and powerful.

I did an internet search of "intrinsic motivation research" and the first three articles were cited in other articles an average of 12,322 times each. The citing goes on and on with 494, 3,439, 1,820, 624, 2,491, 2,868, etc., references for other articles. Existing concurrently with this research is the sad fact that only 5-8% of United States students retain their intrinsic motivation for learning in school for the 12 years after kindergarten. The aim of *How to Create a Perfect School* is not to add to the plethora of intrinsic-motivation documents but to help parents and educators to day by day, week by week, month by month, quarter by quarter, and year by year increase the percentage of students who maintain their kindergarten level of intrinsic motivation all through their K–12 education. If only 1% more US students maintain their intrinsic motivation for all 13 years of K–12 education, that's approximately 50,000 more high school seniors every year who are working very hard in school and receiving great joy from the learning process. We can do far better than 1% improvement. Immeasurably better.

References

_____, (2018) Farnam Street.

Baker, Kevin. (2016) *America the Ingenious*: New York, NY: Artisian.

Batterson, Mark. (2006) *In a Pit with a Lion on a Snowy Day*: Colorado Springs, CO: Multnomah Books.

Batterson, Mark. (2014) *The Circle Maker*: Grand Rapids, MI: Zondervan.

Bordewich, Fergus M. (2016) *The First Congress*. New York, NY: Simon & Schuster.

Byrk, Anthony; Gomez, Louis; Grunrow, Alicia; and LeMahieu, Paul. (2015) *Learning to Improve*. Boston: Harvard Education Publishing

Canfield, Jack. (2015) *The Success Principles*. New York, NY: HarperCollins Publishers.

Clear, James. (2018) *Atomic Habits*. New York, NY: Penguin Random House.

Deming, W. Edwards. (1994) *The New Economics*. Cambridge, MA: MIT Press.

Duckworth, Angela. (2016) *Grit*. New York, NY: Scribner

Dweck, Carol (2006) *Mindset*. New York: Ballantine Books

Fullan, Michael. http://thelearningexchange.ca/wp-content/uploads/2017/03/Fullan-The-Impact-of-Deep-Learning-AODA.pdf

Galesis, Mirta (26 February,2018) "Social circle questions may better predict election outcomes." ScienceDaily, www.sciencedaily.com/releases/2018/02/180226122604.htm

Graham, Billy. (2013) *The Reason for My Hope*. Nashville, TN: The W Publishing Group.

Hattie, John. (2012) *Visible Learning for Teachers*. London: Routledge.

Hattie, John. (2009) *Visible Learning*. London: Routledge.

Hattie, John AC and Conoghue, Gregory M. (August, 2016) "The Science of Learning," www.nature.com/npjscjlearn.

Hattie, John and Gregory C. R. Yates. (2014) *Visible Learning and the Science of How We Learn*: London: Routledge.

Heath, Dan and Chip. (2017) *The Power of Moments*. New York: Simon and Schuster.

Hirsch, E.D. (2006) *The Knowledge Deficit*. New York: Houghton Mifflin.

Jenkins, Lee. (2003) *Improving Student Learning 2nd edition*. Milwaukee: Quality Press

Jenkins, Lee. (2008) *From Systems Thinking to Systemic Action*. Lanham, MD: Rowman & Littlefield

Jenkins, Lee. (2013) *Permission to Forget, 2nd edition*. Milwaukee: Quality Press

Jenkins, Lee. (2016) *Optimize Your School*, Thousand Oaks, CA: Corwin Press

Kramer, Bryan. (2014) *Human to Human: H2H*. San Jose, CA: Pure Matter.

Kramer, Bryan. (2016) *Shareology:* New York, NY: Morgan James Publishing.

Kohn, Alfie. (1993) *Punished by Rewards*. New York, NY: Houghton Mifflin.

Lahey, Jessica. (2015) *The Gift of Failure*. New York, NY: Harper.

Laycock, Mary and Watson, Gene. (1975). *The Fabric of Mathematics*. Hayward, CA: Activity Resources Company.

Martin, Bill Jr. (1972) *Sounds of Language Teacher's Guide*. New York, NY: Hold, Rinehart and Winston.

Marzano, Robert J. (2004) *Building Background Knowledge*. Alexandria, Virginia: ASCD

Maxwell, John. (2007) *The Maxwell Leadership Bible*. Nashville, TN: Thomas Nelson Publishers.

Maxwell, John. (2014) *Good Leaders Ask Great Questions*. New York, NY: Hachette Book Group

McConnaughey, Janyne. (2018) *Brave: A Personal Story of Healing Childhood Trauma*. Greely, CO: Cladach Publishing.

Neufeld, Evelyn. (1972) "Logical Thinking in First Grade Children" University of California, Berkeley Dissertation.

Newmark, Amy and Norville, Deborah. (2016) *The Power of Gratitude*. Chicken Soup for the Soul, LLC.

Orlin, Ben. (2018) *Math with Bad Drawings*. New York, NY: Hachette Book Group.

Pike, Bob. (2015) *Master Trainer Handbook*. Amherst, MA: HRD Press, Inc.

Pink, Daniel. (2009) *Drive*. New York, NY: Riverhead Books.

Pink, Daniel. (2005) *A Whole New Mind*. New York, NY: Riverhead Books.

Thompson, Michael Clay. (1995) *Classics in the Classroom*. Unionville, NY: Royal Fireworks Press.

ABOUT THE AUTHOR

LYLE LEE JENKINS, PH.D., is an author, speaker and recognized authority in improving educational outcomes. He believes that implementing a growth mindset and celebrating progress are the keys to helping students learn more and retain their enthusiasm for school. Lee has spent 50 years in education. Before founding LtoJ Consulting Services in 2003, he worked as a teacher, principal and school superintendent in the California School System and as a university professor.

Lee is the author of *How to Create a Perfect School* and three other books: *Permission to Forget: And Nine Other Root Causes of American's Frustration with Education, Optimize Your School: It's All About the Strategy,* and *From Systems Thinking to Systemic Action.*

Lee's speaking career has taken him across the U.S., and to Latin America, Europe and Asia. In addition, he teaches graduate courses to educators from more than 25 countries. He holds a Bachelor of Arts degree from Point Loma Nazarene University, a Masters of Education from San Jose State University and a Ph.D. from the Claremont Graduate University.

Lee Jenkins' mission is providing practical, proven solutions for the most perplexing education problems. He accomplishes this through writing, speaking and teaching online courses. Lee lives in Scottsdale, Arizona

FREE RESOURCES

Many additional resources to accompany *How to Create a Perfect School* are located at www.LBellJ.com. Examples are key concept lists and blank graphs. These free resources are available for all under the resources tab.

In addition to these free resources are exclusive resources for readers of *How to Create a Perfect School.* They are located at www.LBellJ.com/perfect. These resources are organized by chapters in the book, with one PDF for most chapters. For example, figure 20.4 was printed in the book in black and white. It is located within these exclusive resources in color. Additionally, other examples of Pattern Block art/writing completed by students are posted.

A major advantage of this resource is that it can be updated as new examples and modifications come to my attention. Readers may send suggested resources to info@LyleLeeJenkins.com.

In order to access this exclusive collection go to www.LBellJ.com/perfect and register for your free account. In addition to having access to a wealth of resources, you will be added to Lee Jenkins' email list for education insights.